D1152933

FLY FISHING

CHRIS DAWN

‖ •PARRAGON• ‖

This is a Parragon Book

© Parragon 1999

Parragon
Queen Street House
4 Queen Street
Bath
BA1 1HE

Designed, produced and packaged by
Stonecastle Graphics Ltd
Old Chapel Studio, Plain Road, Marden, Tonbridge,
Kent TN12 9LS, United Kingdom

Edited by Philip de Ste. Croix

All rights reserved. No part of this publication may be
reproduced, stored in a retrieval system, or transmitted in
any way or by any means, electronic, mechanical,
photocopying, recording or otherwise, without the prior
permission of the copyright holder.

ISBN 0 75253-089-5

Printed in Singapore

Photographic credits
l = left, r = right, t = top, b = below

All pictures courtesy of **EMAP (Trout Fisherman)/
Peter Gathercole** with the exception of the following:
R. Calbrade: pages 40*(l)*, 74, 75*(t)*, 78, 79*(t)*.
Russell Symons: page 21*(b)*.
Michael D. Watts: pages 68*(l)*, 69*(b)*.
Robin Griggs: artwork pages 6, 11.

CONTENTS

FLY FISHING

FLY FISHING is regarded by its devotees as the pinnacle of all the angling skills and disciplines. It certainly requires more than a measure of skill when it comes to casting, for the only weight is that of the line itself.

The art comes in persuading the quarry, usually a trout or salmon but increasingly sea fish, to take an artificial fly created from fur, feather and tinsel to represent their natural food. The resultant battle is invariably breathtaking as the angler fights a fish that will run hard and jump high in its efforts to escape. With no gearing in the fly reel to give the angler a technical advantage, the fight is direct between angler and fish.

The philosophy and esoteric delights of fly fishing reach back down the centuries. The method was first described by Claudius Aelianus in the third century AD when he wrote of fishermen in Macedonia winding red wool around their hooks and fastening on 'two feathers that grow under a cock's wattles and which are the colour of dark wax.'

In 1496 Dame Juliana Berners, the Abbess of Sopwell Priory near St Albans in Hertfordshire, wrote about using artificial flies on her local River Ver 150 years before Izaak Walton described trout fishing on the nearby River Lea in

Below: A fly-caught brown trout from Carsington Water, Derbyshire.

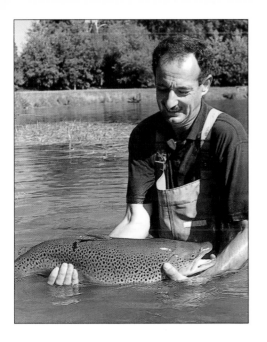

Above: Brown trout are now reared artificially to double figures.

The Compleat Angler. Walton's later friendship with Charles Cotton and their experiences on the River Dove produced a new chapter in a later edition entitled 'Instructions how to angle for trout or grayling in a clear stream.' Modern fly fishing was born.

The purist cult of chalkstream dry fly fishing was started in the late nineteenth century by the great angling writer F. M. Halford, to be challenged this century by such luminaries as G.E.M. Skues and later Frank Sawyer. Skues reasoned that all trout take more of their food from below the surface than from the top. So the deadly art of upstream nymph fishing was born.

River keeper Frank Sawyer built on Skues' pioneering work by developing more general patterns like the world-famous Pheasant Tail Nymph and the technique known as the 'induced take'.

Modern Fly Fishing

In more modern times, English angling writers such as John Goddard, Brian Clarke and Richard Walker have studied the river trout and how it feeds in even greater detail to give us even more deadly methods and flies.

On the stillwater side, the flies and methods remained the same as for rivers until the 1960s, when the opening of a number of large reservoirs in the south of England

made trout fishing available to all. This fast-growing branch of the sport produced its own gurus… anglers like Bob Church, Arthur Cove and John Wadham whose fly patterns and methods are still used and copied today.

But the fly-fishing revolution was not over, as more and more small lakes, ponds and gravel pits were netted to remove coarse fish and then stocked with trout. Even today, there are more small trout fisheries than ever before. And alongside this growth came a wealth of dazzling flies and parallel technical developments in tackle and techniques.

Will the bubble burst? It is doubtful unless global warming makes many shallow southern English waters unsuitable for trout. Fly fishing appeals to all ages and sexes. Even retired couples who have never before held a rod are flocking to take up the sport.

Besides the physical challenge of casting a fly, there is the artistic challenge of first tying it. In addition, trout fisheries by their very nature are usually scenic places, while the sport is generally more sociable than either coarse or sea angling. And there is always the attraction of taking home the catch.

Dame Juliana would not recognize the sport today. But she certainly would have approved.

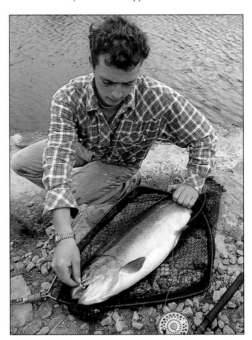

Above: Small-water rainbows are regularly caught to 20lb (9kg).

TACKLE

RODS

F LY RODS have not changed as much in design as their coarse and sea fishing counterparts down the years. The fly angler of yesteryear could pick up today's rod and cast happily with it. What he would notice is the weight difference. Whereas he would have been used to a heavy rod of split cane, or even greenheart, the modern carbon fly rod weighs just a few ounces.

The role of the rod remains the same as it was 100 years ago... to cast the fly-line. So to achieve this, the fly rod must be flexible along its length. However, there is now a marked degree of variation in the action of the rods to suit different casting and fishing styles.

Fast Action

This type of rod has grown in popularity in recent years, thanks to increased sales of American-made rods in the UK. The Americans prefer a rod that is both light and stiff for their fishing where the casting action is in the top joint.

This style of rod, epitomized in brands like Sage and Loomis, is not really best for the beginner. It requires a fast casting action to make it work, and is capable of casting long distances with a narrow line loop. This is ideal for long-range fishing where accuracy is important.

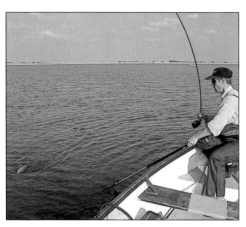

Above: The most popular length for boat rods is 10ft (3m).

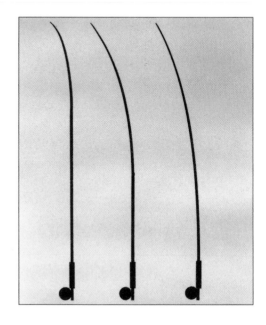

Above: Fast, middle-to-tip and slow rod actions.

Middle to Tip

The action of the vast majority of modern fly rods fall under this description. Here the rod bends from halfway down the blank, under the load of the line, requiring a slower action and a wider line loop which many anglers find easier to achieve.

An angler of average casting ability will be able to cast just as far with this style of rod as with the faster-taper rod. It is only the expert casters who are really able to 'wind up' the fast taper rod to enjoy its maximum potential.

The middle-to-tip action rod can also be easier to fish with at short range as it requires less line out through the rings to get the rod working. The softer tip action acts as a shock absorber allowing the use of lighter leaders.

Slow

This is the soft action of cane fly rods, which is still preferred by some traditionalists. This style of rod is used

Left: A fast-action rod is great for distance casting and hooking fish at long range. This angler is fishing Kingfisher Lake in Herefordshire, and is letting the trout tire itself against the pull of the rod. Below: A softer action is best for stalking fish at close range on clear-water fisheries like Chalk Springs in Sussex. A fine leader can be used without fear of breaking the line.

purely for either river fishing dry fly and nymph, or loch-style fishing at short range.

Not suitable for making long casts, it is ideal for roll casting and for working the flies close to the boat. There is no problem here either with pulling the flies out of the fish's mouth by striking too quickly, or of breaking the leader. The rod just keeps bending.

One disadvantage is that in a strong wind, this type of rod is difficult to hold still.

AFTM Rating

A rod must be correctly matched to the right fly-line for it to cast to its full potential. Use too light a line and there will be insufficient weight to load the rod. Use too heavy a line and the rod will overload. Either way, poor casting distances will result.

Each rod carries an AFTM (Association of Fishing Tackle Manufacturers) line weight number stencilled on its butt joint. Some may give a range of matching line weights, say from 7-9, while others are very specific with, say, a 7 rating. The AFTM numbers describe the weight of a line, calculated in grains along the first 30ft (9m).

Length

River rods are usually short – from six feet up to 8ft 6in (1.8-2.6m), with line ratings from two to six. Overall, a five weight rod would be the average.

Stillwater bank rods range from nine to ten feet (2.7-3m), with nine and a half feet (2.9m) being the most popular length in Europe. American anglers often prefer a shorter rod. Line ratings are from six right up to a nine. Overall, a seven weight would be the average.

For boat fishing, a ten-foot (3m) rod is the most popular but lengths can reach 11ft 6in (3.5m) for traditional loch-style fishing. A lure rod may be rated as a nine, whereas a rod for dry fly would be only a six.

Rings

A fly rod may have hard-chrome double-foot snakes, single-leg snakes or lined guides. The faster-taper, distance-casting rods normally carry the snake rings as favoured on American rods.

REELS

Above: Two state-of-the-art, American-made fly reels from Flylogic, which are now available in Great Britain.

FLY REELS are very collectable items of tackle with antique reels from firms like Hardy, Farlow and Allcock now fetching thousands of pounds at tackle auctions. In many ways, the reels in use today are remarkably similar to the antique reels of the past, working on a simple centre-pin principle. But today's modern technology has created high-performance drag systems using cork or carbon-fibre discs.

The basic fly reel is no more than a storage system for the fly-line. Line to be cast is stripped off by hand, and the fish played by either retrieving or releasing line held in the hand. However, this way of fishing has its problems when a good fish is hooked. The loose coils of line can either catch round a twig or on the bottom of the boat, resulting in a lost fish. Today's modern trout angler prefers to play his fish straight off the reel.

The more basic fly reels rely on a simple check system, while the more expensive use a disc brake. Many of the American-made reels have a very robust drag to cope with the use of either light tippets, or powerful running fish like steelhead or bonefish.

A well-designed reel also needs to have a good line capacity, a counterbalance to minimize spool wobble and an exposed rim for palming the spool. Weight, too, is important, which is why aluminium is a popular material with reel makers. Some reel engineers go to a lot of trouble to ventilate the back to keep the weight down.

Reel Size

As with the line, the reel must match the rod. It is no good putting a heavy, wide-spooled reel on a light river rod, or vice-versa.

River reels (2.75in, 7cm spool) will carry lines from two weight up to a six weight. Reels for lakes, large rivers

POPULAR REELS

Budget – Leeda Rimfly, Leeda Dragonfly, Leeda LC, Lineshooter.

Mid range – Hardy Ultralite, Hardy Marquis, Orvis Battenkill, System 2, Sharpes Menteith, STH.

Top range – Loop, Sage 500, Hardy Sovereign, Charlton Signature, Logic, ATH Rio Orbigo, Abel, Mastery.

Leeda RimFly.

SALTWATER FLY REELS

These really are the top of the range as they need to be built from the very strongest materials to withstand corrosion from salt, and the line-stripping runs of sea fish like tuna, sailfish and dolphin. Most are anti-reverse, meaning that just the centre spool revolves. This allows the angler to set the drag to the critical point at which the fish can take line, while the angler can pump the rod and still recover line. The best models include Henschel, RST, Finn-Nor, Billy Pate.

and small stillwaters (3.25in, 8.25cm spool) will take six and seven weight lines. Reels for reservoir, sea-trout and salmon (4in, 10.2cm spool) require a much larger spool capacity to take lines from eight weight right up to a 12 weight, or even a shooting head.

Most anglers will carry a number of spare spools loaded with different lines that can be quickly and easily changed. Cassette reels like the LC and STH are also growing in popularity.

Do's and Don't's

Always make sure that you have sufficient backing on the reel before you put on the fly-line. You can find this out first by temporarily winding it on over the fly-line until you are near the rim.

Never let your nylon leader get trapped under the coils of fly-line. If you do, it will invariably tangle round the line and cut through it down to the core. Some reels have a groove in which to trap the end of the leader.

When you buy a new reel or rod, it is worth checking first that the reel seat fits your rod handle. Not all are compatible.

Finn-Nor.

Try not to drop the cheaper reels. You can distort the cage so that the spool will no longer freely revolve.

Before you put on the line, check first whether the reel is set up for right- or left-hand retrieve. Most reels can be quickly changed from one configuration to the other, depending upon which hand the the angler prefers to use to play the fish. Traditionally, reels are set up for left-hand wind, but many anglers now prefer to switch over so that they both cast and play the fish with the right arm.

Loop reel.

Hardy Sovereign.

FLY-LINES

THE FLY-LINE supplies the weight that makes it possible to cast a tiny, delicate fly up to 25 yards (23m) or more. Lines are available in a wide range of weights, profiles, densities and colours to match both the rod you are using and the type of fishing you are intending to pursue.

Line Weight

This is calculated in grains over the first 30ft (9.14m) of line. The lighter lines of #2, #3, #4 and #5 are best suited for short casting on rivers where delicacy and accuracy are paramount. Heavier lines of #6, #7, #8 and #9 are best for stillwater fishing where distance casting with larger flies is required, or for sea-trout fishing in fast rivers. Lines of #10 and #12 are used by salmon anglers or saltwater fly anglers casting large, heavy flies.

Line Profile

The first two letters on the manufacturer's box will inform you about the profile of the line. These are normally either WF (weight forward), DT (double taper) or ST (shooting taper).

The most popular line profile for the stillwater angler is undoubtedly the weight-forward line, where the weight of the line is concentrated at the front end to allow long casts to be easily made. This is achieved by making the front taper thicken to a belly, before tapering off again to a thin running line.

Above: Fly-lines are available in a choice of profiles. It is essential that the line is attached to the reel backing the correct way round.

The length of this belly can vary with the type of line that the manufacturer has designed. For a line designed for more delicate fishing, the belly will be around 18ft (5.5m) in length. However, on a line designed for out-and-out distance casting, the belly section may be up to 32ft (9.75m) in length. The overall lengths of lines themselves may also vary from 90ft (27.4m) up to 105ft (32m).

To further confuse the issue of line profiles, manufacturers now talk of rocket tapers, nymph tapers, distance tapers, wind-beater tapers, bonefish tapers and even pike tapers. In addition there are the triangle taper (TT) and arrowhead taper (AT). In reality, they are all types of weight-forward lines supplied with variations in taper length and thickness of tip which are designed to cast heavy flies and overcome any headwind. The description on the box will tell you whether they are suitable for the use you have in mind.

If optimum presentation is the most important aspect to consider, then a double taper line is the one to choose. Equally tapered at either end with the weight in the middle, this type of line is easy to cast and also has the advantage that it can always be reversed when one end wears out. Most river anglers prefer to fish with a double taper line.

Left: This is a weight-forward floating line.

HOW THE LINE CODE WORKS

WF 8 S: the first two letters indicate the profile of the line, the middle number its weight, and the last letter its density.

POPULAR LINE MAKES

Cortland 444, Scientific Anglers Mastery, Airflo 7000 Ts, Lee Wulff Triangle Taper, Air Cel, Wet Cel, Masterline Jubilee.

Right: There are a variety of line profiles, each of which has a different casting property.

The shooting taper, or shooting head, is a very specialized line in which the heavy front taper is spliced to a fine running line of braided nylon. This type of line is only suitable for distance casting and needs a double haul cast to get it out.

Line Density

You can choose from a floating, sink-tip, intermediate, slow-sinking, medium-sinking or fast-sinking line to match the mood and location of the trout. Ideally, the angler will need to have every one of these lines in his tackle bag, but overall the floating line will prove the most versatile for both river and lake fishing.

However, more and more stillwater anglers are now selecting the intermediate line as their first choice. When pulled back quickly, this line will sink sufficiently to fish your flies just under the surface and eliminate the nuisance of wind drag. If left to sink a little longer, you can retrieve the flies on a straight line a foot (30cm) or so below the surface.

As far as sinking lines are concerned, these days there is much more choice than ever before, offering sink rates from as slow as 1in (2.5cm) per second to rates as fast as 7in (17.8cm) per second. Consistently hot summers in recent years have meant that ultra-fast sinking lines, such as the Di-7 or Wet Cel V, are more important than ever in allowing the flies to sink quickly to the cooler depths where feeding trout are to be found.

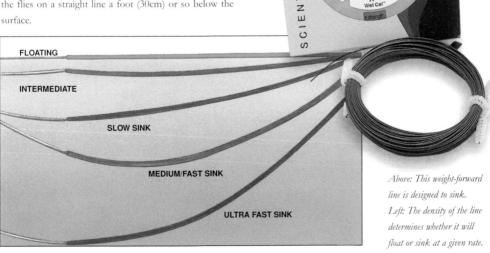

Above: This weight-forward line is designed to sink.

Left: The density of the line determines whether it will float or sink at a given rate.

TOP TIP

When you wind a new fly-line onto the reel, make sure that the line leaves the plastic spool in the same plane as it goes on the reel. If you do not, you will suffer from line twist and 'memory' (coils in the line). Get someone to poke a pencil through the central hole in the plastic spool and let it revolve as you wind the line on to your reel. It is a good idea to stretch the line manually before you cast.

Above: Attach the backing line to the reel by means of a loop. Use sufficient backing so that the fly-line completely fills the spool.

Line Colour

Traditionally only available in white or ivory, modern floating fly-lines are now available in a wide spectrum of colours, many of which make it easier for the angler to see his line. As well as blue, peach and yellow, you can now buy lines in fluorescent orange and vivid green. Sinking lines, however, tend to be in darker colours, while the most popular intermediate line on the market is colourless.

If you are starting fly fishing, there is no need to spend large sums of money on a top-quality imported fly-line. Start off with a budget-priced line from a British manufacturer that has the braided backing already attached. You will need at least 50 yards (45.7m) to ensure that the fly-line fills the reel spool to the lip. Attach the braided backing to the fly-line using either a plastic sleeve and superglue (as with the leader–see page 13), or with a nail knot.

Above: Attach the braided backing to the fly-line using either a nail knot or a plastic sleeve and superglue.

LEADERS

Y OU WILL need a length of nylon, or the more recently introduced braid, between your fly and the fly-line – this is called the leader. The length of the leader can vary from as little as 12in (30cm) to more than 20ft (6m), depending on the type of fishing you are doing. Most importantly, the leader should taper from the initial butt section that is connected to the fly-line to the tippet (see page 14) at the point where the fly is attached. This taper helps the fly to turn over at the end of the cast, and alight delicately on the water.

Leader Makeup

Traditionally, the nylon leader was attached to the end of the fly-line by means of a needle knot, when stiff nylon of, perhaps, 16lb (7.26kg) breaking strain was pushed up into the central core of the fly line for an inch (2.5cm) or so, and then out through a small hole in the side of the line. The nylon was then whipped securely to the fly-line using a spade end or nail knot.

The arrival of the braided loop with its quick and easy method of pushing the fly-line into the hollow end of the braid and then securing it with a purpose-made plastic sleeve and dab of superglue has largely supplanted the

Right: The needle knot.

Left: Attach a braided loop to the end of the fly-line by means of a plastic sleeve and a dab of superglue.

tricky needle knot. However, some anglers still prefer to strip the end of the fly-line of its outer coating and whip a loop in the core in order to attach the leader.

For reservoir fishing, a straight 12ft (3.7m) length of single-strength breaking strain nylon tied to the heavier butt section, or braided loop, will suffice. But better presentation and casting will result by tapering the leader. You can either use a manufacturer's tapered leader, or create your own by stepping down the breaking strain from say 10lb (4.54kg) to 6lb (2.72kg) to 4lb (1.81kg) using either a double blood knot, grinner or a water knot to join the sections of line. Never try to join together two nylons of widely-varying diameters – i.e. 12lb (5.44kg) line to 4lb (1.81kg) line – the knot will not hold.

A tapered leader will transmit the wave of energy sent by you through the rod tip. This energy continues from the tip down the fly-line and tapered leader to the fly, achieving a good, clean turnover. Braided tapered leaders up to 5ft (1.5m) are now gaining in popularity. These are available in slow, medium or even fast-sinking ratings.

Dropper Knots

Boat anglers like to fish with up to three artificial flies attached to their leader, usually spaced 5ft (1.5m) apart giving a total leader length of around 15ft (4.6m) from fly-line to point fly. This part of the leader is made up from a single-strength nylon – usually around 5lb (2.27kg) breaking strain – using water knots to create the droppers to which the flies are attached. As a new length of nylon is tied on, the loose end that hangs downwards becomes the dropper. These may start at up to 6in (15cm) in length, but as flies are discarded and new ones are tied on during the day's fishing, the dropper can end up at half that length.

Never use the loose end of nylon pointing up the line as the dropper. It will snap as soon as a fish is hooked.

Types of Leader

Great advances have been made in nylon leader material in recent years. Dark-coloured nylon is strictly out. Opaque green or colourless leader material is now the first choice for many anglers.

A big breakthrough a few years ago was the introduction of low-diameter, 'double-strength', co-polymer leader material. Although there were problems with it knotting and kinking, it meant that an angler could fish with a leader as fine as conventional 3lb (1.36kg) monofilament line that actually had the strength of 6lb (2.72kg) monofilament. But instead of using the strength advantage, most anglers opted to use the finest diameter lines because they appeared almost invisible to the fish. Hence more fish were hooked, but just as many were lost.

However, the low-diameter co-polymer is deadly on a day of bright sunshine and clear water, especially when just one dry fly is used. But it kinks easily and needs changing far more often than conventional monofilament.

Now there is a new product, fluorocarbon, that may supersede all the others in the manufacture of leaders. Claimed to be invisible in the water due to its light-absorbing properties, it is very expensive in comparison to other leader material. But its use will inevitably spread in the future.

As with double-strength nylon leaders, fluorocarbon must never be knotted to conventional nylon.

Knots

Although the double blood knot and water knot are ideal for joining two sections of nylon, the tucked blood knot or single grinner is best for attaching the fly. The turle knot is also used for attaching dry flies. Always wet the leader

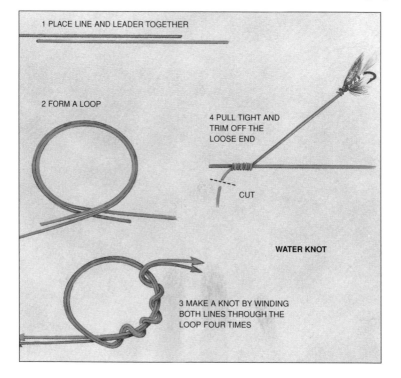

1 PLACE LINE AND LEADER TOGETHER

2 FORM A LOOP

4 PULL TIGHT AND TRIM OFF THE LOOSE END

CUT

WATER KNOT

3 MAKE A KNOT BY WINDING BOTH LINES THROUGH THE LOOP FOUR TIMES

Left: The water knot is useful for creating the droppers that are necessary to attach artificial flies to the leader. Boat anglers often fish with three flies on their line, spaced at intervals of 5ft (1.5m) along the leader. Always use the length of nylon facing down the line for the dropper and carefully trim off the loose end that points up the line.

TOP TIPPET
The flies are attached to a braided leader by means of short lengths of monofilament line called tippets.

before pulling the coils of the knot tight. Then test the knot using a slow pull when you are sure the coils are taut and neatly butting together.

Leader Length

If the fish are fussy on a stillwater, you may need a long leader of up to 25ft (7.6m). However, on a river the leader may be no longer than 9ft (2.7m). For stalking fish, when you need to be able to control the fly very accurately, a short leader of 8 to 10ft (2.4-3m) is all you require. The average reservoir leader is usually around 15ft (4.6m) in length.

Leader Breaking Strain

Always test your nylon before making up a new leader. It may have deteriorated and lost its original breaking strain (bs). It always pays to discard the first foot (30cm) anyway. For river fishing, you may need to go down to 2lb (0.9kg) bs while for most stillwaters, 4lb (1.81kg) bs is as light as it is safe to go.

American brands of leader material still use the X system to denote strength and diameter. For example a 7X tippet would be 2.5lb (1.13kg) bs and .098mm, while a heavier 2X leader would be 7lb (3.18kg) bs and 0.22mm.

DIAMETER COMPARISON OF SOME LEADING BRANDS OF LEADER MATERIAL

Drennan Double Strength 5lb (2.27kg) (0.165mm); Wychwood Subsurface 5lb (2.27kg) (0.22mm); Ashima fluorocarbon 4lb (1.81kg) (0.18mm); Snowbee Magic Line 4lb (1.81kg) (0.148mm); Drennan Subsurface green 4lb (1.81kg) (0.20mm); Maxima 4lb (1.81kg) (0.17mm).

On a rough, windswept day in coloured water when the fish will not notice a heavier line, an angler could happily fish a thicker diameter leader knowing that it is less likely to kink or become damaged than more delicate, finer diameter lines, even if they were of similar breaking strains.

GRINNER KNOT

1 THREAD LINE THROUGH THE EYE

2 PULL THE END BACK ALONG LINE, THEN FORWARD AND LOOP AROUND LINE

3 WIND AROUND FOUR TIMES AND PULL LINE TIGHT

1 THREAD LINE THROUGH THE EYE

2 WRAP END AROUND THE LINE FOUR COMPLETE TURNS

3 BRING THE END THROUGH THE LOOP NEXT TO THE EYE

4 THEN PULL THE END BACK THROUGH ITS OWN LOOP AND PULL TIGHT

TUCKED BLOOD KNOT

The grinner knot (above) or the tucked blood knot (left) are the best methods for attaching the fly to the leader. When tying knots in nylon, always wet the line first and slowly pull the knot tight to avoid damaging it. Ensure that the coils are taut and neatly butting together and you will have a knot that will securely hold a hooked fish.

ACCESSORIES

Left: Choose your accessories wisely and you will avoid the problem of being burdened with an over-heavy tackle bag.

ONE OF THE beauties of fly fishing is that you are able to travel light, but it is easy to become as weighed down with extra rods, reels and bags as the coarse angler. However, there are a number of tackle accessories that are vital to the success of the day, and these should always be part of your kit.

Sunglasses

Never fly fish without the protection of sunglasses. As well as protecting your eyes from the danger of flying hooks, they will also remove the strain of staring at glaring water for hour upon hour. And if you are river fishing or stalking, polarizing sunglasses will allow you to spot fish underwater that you would otherwise be unable to see.

Below: Sunglasses are essential.

Always attach your sunglasses around your neck with a lanyard. Otherwise you will be continually taking them off and putting them down – and maybe even sitting on them!

Priest

Unless you put all of your game fish back, you will need a priest to administer the 'last rites'. Basically a small 'cosh' with a heavy brass head, the priest will kill the fish humanely with one blow to the back of its head. Avoid using sticks, stones or a convenient gatepost to kill your fish. This behaviour is unacceptable, and gives flyfishermen a bad name.

Spoon

Often incorporated into the handle of the priest, a spoon will allow you to see the last meal of the trout you have just dispatched, thus giving you the opportunity of selecting a good imitation fly with which to attract other fish. You simply push the small spoon down the throat of the trout and into its stomach, give it a twist and then withdraw it. The remnants of the meal will be left in the spoon. Identifying the half-digested insects, however, may not be so easy for the inexperienced angler.

Scissors

Scissors are absolutely vital for cutting leaders, changing flies and trimming knot stubs. Most fly anglers keep a small pair either in their fishing vest pocket, or on an elasticated extendible zinger so that they are always ready for action.

Forceps

It can sometimes be quite hard to remove a fly from a trout's bony mouth, especially if the fish has swallowed it. A pair of long-nosed forceps allows you to rescue the fly and quickly unhook the trout.

Right: Forceps will make it easy to remove your fly hooks.

Bass Bag

Trout are a soft-fleshed fish and can quickly deteriorate if left exposed to either sun or wind. A well-ventilated bass bag to hold the dead fish can be left either hanging over the side of the boat, or in the lake or river margins.

A useful tip is always to remember to wash out the bag when you get home – otherwise it will smell very fishy.

Floatant

A necessity for dry-fly fishing, floatant is available in a wide variety of forms. River anglers often prefer to use it in spray form, while stillwater fishermen use a gel which is applied with the fingers. But only use the minimum you can get away with.

Sinkant

Just as essential as flotant is a paste that removes any grease and shine from the leader, allowing it to cut through the surface film of the water and sink. When dry-fly or nymph fishing, you may need to degrease the leader several times during the day.

Heavy Metal

This tungsten-impregnated putty can be quickly rolled into small balls which can be added to the fly or leader to make them sink faster.

Indicators

Indicators have been used on rivers for many years, and there is now a growing trend to use them when stillwater fishing. They can be simply a small tuft of fluorescent wool hitched into the leader, a small sticky-backed foam patch or a piece of brightly coloured floating 'dough' pressed on the line. Whichever method you employ, it will indicate a take from a trout which you otherwise might never spot. Sight indicators are banned in competitions.

Spare Line

During the day you may have to remake your leader several times. So you will always need to carry several spare spools of monofilament line in various breaking strains. These are usually sold in 25m and 50m spools especially for the flyfishermen.

Fly Boxes

Do not get bogged down with carrying giant fly boxes crammed with every pattern you own. Instead, break your fly patterns down into dries, nymphs, wets, lures etc, and put them into small boxes that can be carried easily in your waistcoat pockets.

Landing Net

Landing nets come in many shapes and sizes, from the giant Gye net which is slung across the shoulders on a leather strap to the small folding river net that is hung from the waistcoat. Boat anglers prefer to use a wider rigid net attached to a long handle. Whatever style of net you buy, make sure that the mesh is knotless so that the fish can be returned unharmed on catch-and-release waters.

Bag

You will need to put all your accessories into a bag. There are many on the market, including some oversize ones for boat fishing. Choose a well-stitched waterproof bag that is comfortable to carry, and make sure it has sufficient pockets to accommodate all your extras.

Right: Always choose a landing net that has a knotless mesh to avoid damaging the fish.

THE FLY

NATURAL INSECTS

THE WHOLE art of fly fishing is based around successfully imitating the game fish's natural food. And for the various species of trout, the selection is almost endless. Here are some of the major natural food sources for the trout which anglers copy with their artificial flies.

Upwinged Flies *(Ephemeroptera)*
Arguably the most important group of flies for the river fisherman, these are the only ones that have two large upright wings and two or three large tails; they vary in size from the mayfly to the tiny olives. Their miraculous life cycle provides the flyfisherman with all sorts of opportunities for different techniques and patterns.

Above: The mayfly is one of the best known, and largest, of the upwinged flies.

Above right: The spent mayfly spinner provides a ready evening meal for hungry trout.

The richest variety of upwinged flies are generally found on the chalkstreams, but both freestone rivers and large lakes also enjoy hatches of upwings through the year. Indeed some blue-winged olives will hatch out even in the middle of winter.

The eggs laid in the water by the female hatch into nymphs, which spend a year attaining maturity. Different species of nymphs adopt different life styles. For example there are stone clingers, moss creepers, agile darters, silt crawlers and laboured swimmers – all of which perfectly describe their habitats and lifestyles.

Eventually the time comes for the nymph to hatch into the dun (sub imago) with its dull wings. Yet within a day, this fly will change again into the sparkling spinner (imago) and be ready to mate. The female then returns to the water to lay her eggs, dies and falls on the water in the evening as the spent spinner, at which time the trout may start to feed heavily on the dying insects. The brief life of these flies gives rise to the word 'ephemeral'.

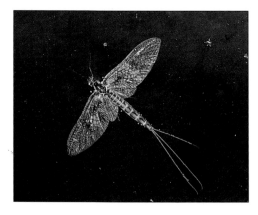

UPWINGED SPECIES
Claret dun/spinner, sepia dun/spinner, mayfly (*danica* and *vulgata* species), blue-winged olive, march brown, yellow may, large dark olive, medium olive; small dark olive, pale watery, iron blue, pond olive, lake olive, pale evening dun.

SEDGE FLY SPECIES

Silver sedge, brown sedge, grannom, silverhorn, grouse-wing, small red sedge, great red sedge, caperer, cinnamon sedge, *rhyacophila*, *hydropsyche* (both free swimming).

Sedge Flies *(Trichoptera)*

The Latin name for these flies translates literally as 'hair wing' which describes the tiny hairs on their wings, but it is the roof shape of the adult's wings that is most noticeable to the angler.

Known in America more widely as caddis flies, their larvae, which live in silt or gravel bottoms, are a significant food source for trout in stillwaters, chalkstreams and freestone rivers. Years ago, caddis larvae were a popular bait for trout.

The larvae's best-known habit is building a case from tiny pieces of material found underwater to protect itself from predators. All sorts of 'building materials' are used to construct the case, including gravel, sand, small stones, sticks, discarded shells, leaves, reed stems and other vegetable matter. Other forms of caddis larvae are either free-swimming, or they construct a purse or tube-like shelter as a home.

Most larvae complete their life cycle within a year, with the pupa then swimming to the surface or shore to hatch into the adult fly, which can live for up to a week.

Many of the larger species of sedge – there are nearly 200 in the British Isles alone – hatch in the late evening, but it is the pupal stage that is taken most often by the trout. However, there are fly patterns to imitate all stages of the life cycle.

Above left: A wide variety of upwinged flies, such as this pond olive, provide a good supply of food for trout.

Above: This pond olive nymph will turn into a winged dun and then, within a day, into the adult spinner.

Stoneflies *(Plecoptera)*

Although there are only around 30 British species, the stoneflies, or hard-winged flies, are important to both river angler and trout on freestone rivers in Wales and the north of England. As their name suggests, their preferred habitats are fast rivers with stony or rocky beds, although they are also found along stony lake shores.

Stonefly nymphs may be as long as two inches (5cm), and go through a number of instars (changes of outer skin). Their strong bodies and flattened wing cases are built to withstand the fast-flowing river environment among the rocks. Stoneflies are often referred to as 'creepers' in the north of England.

The adult is of importance to the fly angler only when the female returns to the water to deposit her eggs. At that time the trout will often take the egg-laying female or the spent fly.

Flat-winged Flies *(Diptera)*

This is easily the largest Order of flies, containing many thousands of different species, all of which are important to the trout.

For the flyfisher, especially on stillwaters, it is the massive non-biting midge or buzzer *(Chironomids)* family that is of most interest, particularly those species with an aquatic life cycle. Huge hatches occur on lakes and reservoirs from spring to autumn with the trout targeting various stages in their development.

The larval stage, or bloodworm, live in tubes buried in silt or mud. Their colour can vary widely from blood red, due to the presence of haemoglobin, through to green and brown. Trout take them avidly when they leave their burrows to feed. A favourite bait for coarse fishermen, bloodworm imitations can also be deadly for the fly angler.

The next stage is the pupa, which lasts between 36 and 72 hours. When the pupa is ready to hatch, it swims to the surface. And it is at this stage when it is most vulnerable to the trout.

Top: The pupa of the buzzer swims to the surface of the water when it is about to hatch.

Above: The hawthorn fly is easily identified by its black body and long trailing legs.

The trout will often start by feeding deep on buzzer pupa, picking them off several feet down as they start their hazardous ascent to the surface. This is when a weighted Buzzer pattern is required. The colour of the midge pupae can vary from black through to olive, brown and red. And different-coloured patterns will be needed to attract the trout.

If the hatching insect cannot break through the surface tension of the water, it is at the trout's mercy and can produce a heavy surface rise with the trout 'head and

> **MIDGES**
>
> Ginger midge, olive midge, duck fly (Blae & Black), Blagdon green midge, red midge, brown midge, grey boy, black midge.

tailing'. This can be particularly evident in areas of calm water like a wind lane where the buzzer pupa get trapped. A study of this feeding pattern has led to the development of many interesting fly patterns, such as Emergers and Suspender Buzzers, that are fished right in the surface film.

Trout will also happily take the adult fly, which can appear in dense clouds over the tops of trees looking like a column of smoke. The buzzing noise of the females as they return to lay their eggs gives rise to the name buzzer.

In recent years, midge hatches have become more important on rivers, especially where water quality has declined and more silting has occurred.

Terrestrial Flies

A variety of flies are blown onto the water during the year, and if there are enough of them they may start a rise. The hawthorn fly *(Bibio marci)* or St Mark's fly usually appears towards the end of April, and is easily identified by its long trailing legs.

A similar fly in moorland areas is the heather fly *(Bibio pomonae)*. It also has long trailing legs, bright red at the tops, and can swarm in mid-summer. Look out, too, for the black and yellow banded drone fly, cow dung fly and even the bluebottle. All will be taken with relish by the trout in high summer.

In autumn, the cranefly or daddy longlegs can appear in numbers and be blown onto the lakes. Their gangling legs seem a magnet for trout, who take them avidly from the surface. In Ireland, they dap with live craneflies which are allowed to drift across the waves using a floss line.

Damselflies *(Zygoptera)*

Although there are 17 British species of this familiar aquatic fly, it is the blue damsel and the green agrion that will be most familiar to the flyfisher, as they hover and dart across the lakes and rivers in summer. The sinuous movement of the nymph attracts the trout as it swims towards the shore to hatch into the handsome adult. Many stillwater patterns are based around imitating the nymph which can vary in colour from dark brown to bright green.

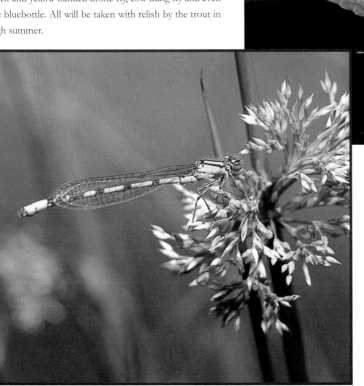

Above: The damsel nymph lives in the water of rivers and lakes until it is ready to hatch into the winged adult. There are many artificial patterns that are designed to imitate the nymph, which can vary in colour from green to dark brown.

Left: The adult blue damsel is a handsome insect that darts and hovers over the water in summer. It is a familiar sight to any angler.

Beetles *(Coleoptera)*

All types of beetles can end up on the surface of the water, especially on rivers where they fall from bankside vegetation. Small floating beetle patterns can be deadly.

In upland areas like Wales, Scotland and the West Country, the coch y bonddu beetle can be encountered in large swarms during June. And when they are blown onto the water, they can produce a good rise. The traditional Welsh fly to imitate it is known as the Coch-y-Bonddu, and can be fished wet or dry. Another beetle that can produce large summer rises on the English reservoirs is the rape seed beetle.

Other Aquatic Life

Daphnia: These tiny crustaceans, also known as water fleas, swarm in vast underwater clouds in stillwaters and form the staple diet of many deep-feeding trout. They can be so plentiful at times that the trout never bother to come to the surface to feed. The daphnia move up and down in the water depending on the sunlight and time of day. So it is important for the angler to find the depth at which the trout are feeding on them. Although they are too small to imitate individually, a brightly coloured orange lure pulled quickly through the shoal will take daphnia-feeding fish.

Freshwater shrimps: Extremely common in both still and running water, shrimps are greedily gobbled up by trout wherever they find them. It is common to see trout picking them out of the bottom gravel or moss in clear rivers or the margins of lakes, hence the wide success of the leaded Shrimp pattern.

Corixa: More commonly known as the lesser water boatman, these small creatures are found in lakes and some rivers. They haunt the weedy shallows as they have to make constant journeys to the surface to replenish their oxygen bubble. Reservoir trout feed heavily on corixa in late summer and autumn when they shed their skin and take to the air to mate.

Water snails: Trout can become preoccupied with snail feeding, especially with the wandering snail when it floats in vast numbers to migrate to a different area of the lake or reservoir. These fish can be hard to tempt, but there are specialist patterns, such as the Floating Snail or the Black & Peacock Spider, which are often successful. At other times snails are picked off the weed by browsing trout. Snail-feeding gives the trout flesh a good, healthy pink colour.

Above: Daphnia are tiny zooplankton which often thrive in vast underwater clouds. Where daphnia are plentiful, trout sometimes feed on them almost exclusively and will hardly bother to rise to the surface to take flies.
Left: Corixa, often known as the lesser water boatman, are eaten by trout in late summer and autumn as they swarm around the weed beds.

Hog louse: Another crustacean similar to the shrimp, the *Asellus* hog louse is abundant in the muddy margins of lakes and ponds among rotting vegetation. It is often sought in winter by trout when little other food is available.

Fry: Trout are natural predators and will quickly turn to coarse fish fry in late summer and autumn. As the young roach pack together into vast shoals around jetties and pontoons, so both brown and rainbow trout will shoal up and attack the small fish.

Many of their attacks simply leave the young fish stunned on the surface, where the trout can mop them up at their leisure. A whole series of Floating Fry and surface disturbance patterns have been developed to take these fry-feeding fish, which are often specimen trout. A good clue to the presence of fry feeding are seagulls hovering excitedly over the water, waiting to share in the harvest of stunned fish.

Reservoir trout can become preoccupied with 'pin' fry an inch (2.54cm) or so long in late summer, only preying on larger fish as the year progresses. It is always important to ensure that your fry imitation is a similar size to the real thing.

Above: The contents of this trout's stomach indicate that it had been eating roach fry.

Below: Snails can become a favourite food of trout, making the fish hard to tempt on a fly.

RIVER FRY

Trout also feed on small fish, such as minnows, sticklebacks and bullheads, which are found in rivers. Some of the largest brown trout caught from running water are taken on imitative flies like the the Muddler Minnow or Sculpin Minnow.

FLY TYING

THERE IS no greater satisfaction in game fishing than catching a fish on a fly that you have tied yourself. Today much of the mystery of this esoteric art has been removed. There are books, magazines, videos and even night classes to show you how to tie even the most complex patterns.

Fly-tying clubs have sprung up around the world, often swapping patterns on the Internet. There is a wealth of new man-made materials constantly appearing on the market, many items arriving in the UK from overseas. Fly tying is now truly a global pastime.

Starting Off

First you will need to create an uncluttered work area, where you can tie and experiment undisturbed. It will need to be well lit to avoid you suffering from eyestrain. A good portable angled bench light will be invaluable, as will a properly adjustable chair, preferably with arm rests to support your elbows.

Some flyfishermen are lucky enough to have their own fly-tying rooms and benches, but most of us have to make do with a corner of the kitchen table. But make sure before you start that the table you plan to use will accept the clamp of the vice.

Below: Choose the best tools that you can afford – they will help to ensure that you tie the finest flies as your skill develops.

The Tools

Beware of scrimping by buying a cheap vice, as it may not hold the hook securely. There are many types of vice on the market, but you will not go wrong with a simple lever-action model with hardened steel jaws and an adjustable stem.

You will also need two pairs of scissors – one with wide straight blades and a second with curved blades. Keep the first pair for cutting hard materials like tinsel and wire. The second pair can then be saved for finer work such as trimming. The blades need to be fine and very sharp. Again, buy the best you can afford.

The next item you will need are hackle pliers, which are available in a variety of sizes. The jaws should meet evenly and be smooth enough not to cut the hackle feather you will be winding.

You should also buy a spigot bobbin holder, which is a pair of sprung wire arms to hold the bobbin, and a hollow tube through which to feed the thread. The weight of the bobbin holder keeps the thread taut, while the sprung arms maintain sufficient tension on the bobbin to prevent it unwinding.

Finally, you will need a dubbing needle to apply varnish and to pick out the fibres on the body. You may also need a whip-finish tool if you find finishing the fly at the head by hand too difficult.

TOP TIP
Keep all your materials properly stored and well sealed – especially the natural ones which can be eaten by household pests.
A properly organized fly-tying cabinet will eventually seem more than just a good idea.

Right: There is an amazing variety of materials readily available from tackle shops and through mail order.

Hooks

A huge variety of fly hooks are available from a number of different manufacturers. The chemically sharpened hooks from the Far East have grown in popularity, but many tyers still prefer to use the more expensive, but strong, hand-made British hooks.

Fly hooks are usually sold as wet-fly, nymph, shrimp, dry-fly and longshank streamer models. Sizes can range from a large size 4 right down to a tiny 24, depending upon the type of fly you are tying.

Some wet-fly hooks are heavier in the wire and therefore sink faster. Others are offset or curved to help form the shape of the shrimp, grub or pupa being tied. The best bet is to get hold of a catalogue from a hook company and see what is available.

Materials

A visit to your local fly-tackle shop, or a glance through a mail order catalogue, will show you the amazing variety of materials available. But again, it pays to buy the best you can afford, as the cheaper, lower-grade materials can be difficult to use successfully.

If you can afford to, buy a good quality cock cape for your hackle feathers, although the very-best genetically produced capes from America are expensive. The capes will provide hackle feathers in all sizes, right down to dry flies as small as size 28. They are also available in all the various colours, including such famous shades as Iron Blue Dun, Honey Dun, Cree, Badger, Grizzle and Furnace. A cheaper alternative is to buy an Indian or Chinese cape, natural and dyed.

The list of other materials you may eventually need is endless, but natural products like seal's fur, rabbit's fur, hare mask, mole skin, marabou, pheasant, squirrel tail, calf tail, bucktail, partridge, golden pheasant, mallard, teal and *cul de canard* will be essential.

You will also need a selection of man-made body materials like chenille, yarn, wool, foam, Antron, Hareton, SLF, and Nymph Glass, plus various threads, tinsels, flosses and wire for ribbing.

Keep all your materials properly stored and well sealed – especially the natural ones which can be eaten by household pests. A properly organized fly-tying cabinet will eventually seem more than just a good idea.

Right: Fly tying is a combination of science and art. There are books, magazines, videos and night classes that will get you started.

DRY FLIES

THIS IS A fly dressed to float on the surface of the water. The classic river patterns, some of which are more than 100 years old, achieve this by resting on their stiff hackles and tail, which in length should be one and a half to twice the hook gape. Wings were traditionally tied from matched slips of quill feather placed back to back, but a number of other feather materials are now used, including hackle points and hackle fibres. Wings tied from buoyant materials like elk hair, bucktail, polypropylene, antron, foam and *cul de canard* all help the modern dry fly to stay afloat.

The dry fly represents the adult stage of water insects such as olives, mayflies, sedges and midges, plus all the various terrestrials that can be blown on the water.

Emergers

The tension in the surface of the water creates a barrier that the insect must cross as it changes from pupa to adult. It is in this hatching, or emerging, stage that it is most vulnerable to the trout. Many of today's most successful surface flies are actually emerger patterns that sit in, rather than on, the surface.

Floating Adults

On dry, bright days when flies are hatching swiftly and flying away, the full-hackle high-riding patterns work best. However, on damp days the duns' wings take longer to dry and a low-riding pattern will work better. Light dressings are used for flies in calm water, while rougher, heavier water demands a heavier-hackled fly.

Spent Flies

Once their egg-laying is finished, the female spinners become trapped in the surface film and drift away at the mercy of the trout. Spent flies imitate this stage of the life cycle, although trout preoccupied with spinners can be extremely selective.

Collar Hackles

The collar style is the standard method for hackling most dry flies. Birds are reared specially for the purpose of providing feathers for these cock hackles, with two of the best-known producers being Hoffman and Metz. These top-quality genetically-produced capes contain hundreds of hackle feathers for tying all the different size of dry flies.

Above: This Mayfly pattern imitates accurately the adult insect and is designed to float on the surface of the water.

Parachute Hackles

In this style, the hackle is wound around a small projection from the top of the hook. This ensures that the body of the dry fly sits right in or just below the surface film, making it ideal for hackling spent and emerger patterns.

Right: A parachute Pheasant Tail.

Famous Dry Flies

Grey Wulff

Hook: 12/16
Thread: Black
Tail: Bucktail
Body: Grey rabbit fur
Wing: Bucktail
Hackle: Blue dun cock

The classic American dry fly for fast, rough water. Also useful as a mayfly imitation in the larger sizes.

CDC Dun

Hook: 14/20
Thread: Olive
Tail: Blue dun cock hackle fibres
Body: Light olive dubbing blend
Wing: Natural grey cul de canard fibres
Hackle: Cul de canard

Excellent imitation when trout are rising to adult pond and lake olives. Works on river and stillwater.

Grey Duster

Hook: 10/14
Thread: Brown
Tail: Badger cock hackle fibres
Body: Blue-grey rabbit fur
Hackle: Badger cock

Killing general utility dry for trout and grayling which represents a wide selection of insects throughout the season.

Elk Hair Caddis

Hook: 8/10
Thread: Brown
Body: Olive dubbing
Wing: Natural elk hair
Hackle: Palmered brown cock

A pattern for both running and stillwater when the adult caddis are present during late evening and returning to the water to lay their eggs.

Adams

Hook: 14/22
Thread: Grey
Tail: Grizzle hackle fibres
Body: Blue-grey dubbed wool or fur
Wing: Grizzle hackle tips
Hackle: Grizzle cock

Another all-round general-purpose dry fly from America invented by Ray Bergman.

Hare's Ear Suspender

Hook: 12/16
Thread: Olive
Tag: Fluoro green floss
Rib: Fine pearl Lurex
Body: Hare's fur
Thorax: Hare's fur
Head: Grey foam

A modern suspender pattern developed at Rutland Water by John Maitland for taking selective surface-feeding trout.

WET FLIES

THE WET fly is designed to sink just below the surface and imitate the hatching fly. Either hackled or winged, the traditional wet fly is designed to fish either in a team of three on stillwaters, or on fast northern and western streams.

The traditional method of winging wet flies uses two matched slips of quill feather placed back to back. At one time the feathers from many types of birds were used, but now mallard feathers have replaced them.

Winged wet flies are usually fished on the point and middle droppers of a three-fly cast, with a palmered wet fly on the top dropper to create disturbance on the surface.

They are also widely used for sea trout in lochs and rivers. Famous sea-trout wet-fly patterns are the Wickham's Fancy, Bloody Butcher, Alexandra and Silver Invicta.

Below: Wet flies are successful on a wide range of waters, from streams and rivers to lakes and reservoirs, where they are fished just below the surface of the water to imitate hatching flies. This is a Wickham's Fancy, a famous pattern designed for sea-trout fishing.

Palmered Hackles

The palmer style of fly, where the hackle feather is wound down the hook shank, creates a dense, bushy pattern that works perfectly in wave conditions on lochs and reservoirs. This type of wet fly brings the wild brown trout up to the top as it creates its sub-surface disturbance. Underwater the hackles create their own footprints which resemble the feet and legs of an insect blown onto the water.

Even more heavily-palmered patterns, like the Loch Ordie, are used for dapping, especially on Scottish sea-trout lochs.

Soft Hackles

The soft, supple body feathers of gamebirds like grouse, snipe, woodcock and partridge are used as wet-fly hackles in a number of traditional North Country Spider patterns. These soft feathers are very mobile and pulsate in the rough water of the northern streams.

Typical river wet flies are Snipe and Purple, Partridge and Orange, Woodcock and Green, Waterhen Bloa and Dark Watchet.

Famous Wet Flies

Teal, Blue & Silver

Hook: 8/14

Thread: Black

Tail: Golden pheasant tippet

Body: Flat silver tinsel

Rib: Fine silver wire

Wing: Teal flank feather

Hackle: Bright blue cock

Originally created as a sea-trout river pattern, the silver body and barred wing create a good fry imitation for stillwater.

Greenwell's Glory

Hook: 10/16

Thread: Yellow

Tail: Brown partridge

Body: Yellow waxed silk

Rib: Gold wire

Wing: Starling

Hackle: Light furnace

The most famous of all British flies, developed for the River Tweed by Canon Greenwell in 1854. Still as effective today during a hatch of olives on river or lake.

Silver Invicta

Hook: 10/14

Thread: Black

Tail: Golden pheasant crest feather

Body: Flat silver tinsel

Wing: Hen pheasant

Hackle: Natural light red palmered with blue jay at head.

The silver-bodied version of the standard Invicta, this is a deadly summer fly when fished on the point, particularly when trout are on pinfry.

Blae and Black

Hook: 12/16

Thread: Black

Tail: Golden pheasant tippet

Body: Black tying silk

Rib: Oval silver tinsel

Wing: Grey duck or starling

Hackle: Black hen

Another traditional Scottish pattern that represents the duck fly, the large black midge found in Scottish lochs and Irish loughs.

Mallard & Claret

Hook: 10/14

Thread: Brown

Tail: Golden pheasant tippet

Body: Claret seal's fur

Rib: Fine gold wire

Wing: Brown mallard

Hackle: Natural light hen

A classic all-round Scottish wet fly that takes fish from both stream and lake. At its best on a windy, overcast day on the point of a three-fly cast.

Golden Olive Bumble

Hook: 8/12

Thread: Black

Tail: Golden pheasant crest feather

Body: Golden olive seal's fur

Rib: Gold lurex

Hackle: Heavily palmered olive cock and blue jay at head

A classic Irish wake fly that's especially effective at mayfly time due to its body colour. Use on the top dropper in a big wave.

NYMPHS

IN FLY-TYING terms the name 'nymph' covers a massive range of flies from heavily leaded longshank patterns that fish close to the bottom, to tiny river patterns that are fished upstream on a dead drift. Some so-called nymphs for stillwater are really no more than lures, while others are genuine artificial recreations of the aquatic insect.

Nymphs can imitate every stage of invertebrate life underwater, including larvae, nymphs, pupae, shrimps, corixa and even hoglouse. They are usually most effective when fished very slowly. For every floating insect taken by a trout, many more food forms will be consumed under the surface.

Weighting

Nymphs can be either weighted or unweighted depending on the depth at which you want to fish. Many anglers mark the heads of the weighted nymphs in their boxes to distinguish them from the unweighted versions of the same fly.

Weight can be added in various ways, including winding lead wire round the hook shank before you start to tie the fly. Lead wire can also be added to the sides of the hook shank, making it ideal for flat-bodied patterns like Stonefly nymphs.

For really heavy stalking patterns, where the fly must sink quickly, lead foil is used. You can use the foil from round the neck of a bottle of quality wine to this end.

Some stalking patterns are little more than lead wire wrapped around a hook. Such a thin profile means the 'fly' cuts through the water like a knife through butter to reach the fish. Some patterns, such as the Red Hook, are actually no more than a heavy-wired hook painted red!

For delicate river patterns, where the nymph wants to fish just beneath the surface, copper wire is used for weight. This is particularly suitable for very tiny nymphs, such as the ephemerids, which the trout will take just below the surface.

Goldheads

One of the biggest trends in fly tying in recent years has been to add a goldbead head to many patterns. Not only does this provide weight, but it also provides extra flash. Goldhead nymphs are deadly for trout and grayling on rivers where they are permitted, often replacing the more traditional flies.

Silver beads can also be added, while new from America are extra-heavy tungsten beads. There are also tungsten sleeves which can be first slid onto the hook of the tiniest nymph before tying.

Goldheads have become a growing nymph-fishing trend in recent years, often replacing traditional fly patterns. This example is a Black Nugget.

Some Famous Nymphs

Walker's Mayfly

Hook:	Size 8/12 ls
Thread:	Brown
Tail:	Brown pheasant tail
Body:	Pale yellow Angora wool
Underbody:	Lead foil
Rib:	Pheasant tail fibres
Thorax:	Pheasant tail fibres
Wingcase:	Pheasant tail fibres
Legs:	Cock pheasant tail fibres

Classic pattern for rivers and lakes created by the famous English angler Richard Walker. Works well as stalking bug even when no mayfly are hatching.

Montana

Hook:	Size 6/14 ls
Thread:	Black
Tail:	Cock hackle fibres
Body:	Black chenille (lead can be added first)
Thorax:	Lime-green chenille
Wingcase:	Black chenille
Legs:	Black cock

American pattern now used worldwide. Very effective for stillwater trout when heavily leaded.

Pheasant Tail

Hook:	Size 10/14 ls
Thread:	Brown
Tail:	Pheasant tail fibres
Underbody:	Copper wire
Overbody:	Pheasant tail fibres
Rib:	Copper wire
Thorax:	Orange seal fur
Wingcase:	Pheasant tail fibres
Hackle:	Natural red game cock

World-famous pattern deadly on river or lake. This stillwater version fished on a long leader imitates a wide range of general nymphs, and even small fish.

Daiwl Bach

Hook:	Size 10/12
Thread:	Silk
Tail:	Brown fibres
Body:	Peacock herl
Hackle:	Hen

A very effective reservoir pattern created by Welsh anglers for Chew and Blagdon.

Killer Bug

Hook:	Size 10/16
Body:	Underbody of lead wire overlaid with three layers of beige darning wool. Use fine copper wire to tie in materials

Invented by chalkstream legend Frank Sawyer, there are few more deadly river patterns than this.

Holographic Buzzer

Hook:	Heavyweight size 10/12
Thread:	Black
Body:	Holographic tinsel
Rib:	Black tying thread coated with clear epoxy or varnish
Thorax:	Black goose biot
Wingcase:	Orange tee-shirt paint
Breathing filaments:	White cul de canard

Buzzer patterns are continually developing. The latest are the fast-sinking slim-line nymphs created from epoxy or varnish like this tying from Peter Gathercole.

STREAMERS AND LURES

GENERALLY TIED to imitate small baitfish, there are more types and styles of lures than any other fly. They can range from the competition angler's mini-lure, tied on a short-shank size 10 hook, to massive tandems on 2/0 hooks for giant brown trout, salmon, pike and saltwater fish.

For lures to work properly, they need to imitate the flash, colour and movement of small prey fish. This is achieved by the choice of materials, they way they are tied on the hook, and how they are fished. Sometimes the lure will need to ripped back as fast as possible. But on other days, it can be fished as slowly as possible.

Movement

The importance of using marabou for both the wings and tails of lures cannot be underestimated. Its undulating action underwater is so alive that it has largely replaced other more traditional winging materials like cock feather, goat hair, squirrel, buck and calf tail.

However, modern man-made materials like Crystal Hair, Pearl Mobile and Twinkle are now being added to wings and tails to create more flash.

Salmon Flies

The modern salmon fly has changed a lot from the complex, fully dressed masterpiece of yesteryear. Hairwing patterns, Waddingtons and tubes, along with shrimp and prawn imitations, are now the standard fare on most famous rivers.

Waddingtons are articulated where the eye of the treble joins the shank of the hook. Tubes are either brass, aluminium or plastic.

Salmon flies for low-water summer conditions are small and sparsely dressed when compared to the heavy tube patterns used early and late in the season. Here are two modern popular Scottish salmon flies:

Below: The Muddler Minnow lure with its clipped deer-hair head.

Some Famous Salmon Flies

Garry Dog

Hook:	6/12 double
Thread:	Black
Body:	Black floss
Rib:	Oval silver
Wing:	Yellow dyed squirrel hair over red
Hackle:	Dyed dark-blue guineafowl

Famous Scottish pattern, particularly effective on rivers that carry a peat stain.

Willie Gunn Tube

Hook:	Treble size 4/10
Thread:	Black
Body:	Black floss
Rib:	Gold
Wing:	Orange and yellow bucktail with spare black

An early-season pattern for heavily peat-stained rivers.

Some Famous Lures

Appetiser

Hook:	Size 8/12
Thread:	Black
Tail:	Orange and green hackle fibres
Body:	White chenille
Rib:	Flat silver tinsel
Wing:	Squirrel and marabou
Throat hackle:	As for tail

A classic reservoir lure devised by Northampton's Bob Church for fry feeders. Can be tied small on competition-sized hooks or as a tandem for deep fishing.

Orange Leadhead

Hook:	Size 8/12
Thread:	Orange
Tail:	Orange marabou
Body:	Orange chenille
Hackle:	Grizzle
Head:	Non-toxic shot

The late Trevor Housby introduced this style of fly onto British waters in the 1970s with devastating results. First known as the Dog Nobbler, its diving action due to the weight at the head is absolutely deadly.

Yellow Booby

Hook:	Size 8/12 wide gaped
Thread:	White
Tail:	Yellow marabou
Body:	Yellow fluoro chenille
Eyes:	Yellow plastazote

A buoyant reservoir pattern which works best when fished deep with a short leader on a fast-sinking line. But also works as a disturbance pattern when fished on the surface. Banned on many catch and release waters. First devised by Gordon Fraser for Eyebrook, and later developed by Mick Bewick for Queen Mother Reservoir, London.

Goldhead Damsel

Hook:	8/10
Thread:	Olive
Tail:	Golden olive marabou
Body:	Golden olive marabou (dubbed)
Body hackle:	Golden olive cock
Rib:	Fine gold wire
Hackle:	Grey partridge dyed golden olive
Head:	Gold bead

Although the Damsel imitations imitate the nymphs of the natural fly, they also work as lures and will take fish from any water at any time. This version of this ever-popular fly is by Kevin Hart.

SPECIES

THE GAME FISH

THANKS TO their desirability both as a source of sport and food, the *salmonidae* family of fish are the best known in the world. Although they originate in the northern temperate zones of Europe, Asia and North America, *salmonids* have been stocked around the globe in suitable clear cool water.

One of the diagnostic features of the *salmonids* is the small adipose fin situated between the dorsal fin and the tail. Spots are another feature, while juvenile fish bear the characteristic parr marks along their sides.

All are predatory, feeding both on invertebrates and fish, often changing diet as they grow larger. They are also longlived with char reaching ages of more than 35 years.

All the members of the *salmonid* family spawn in running water, even though some species like the salmon and sea trout spend much of their lives at sea. They can adapt to either environment.

Their value as a food source has meant that man has hunted them for centuries, but diminishing stocks has seen them farmed artificially. Rainbow trout are produced for the table in huge numbers at fish farms up and down the British Isles. They still need fresh, running water to grow, but their waste affects the rivers that feed the farms.

Rainbow trout have escaped into many natural brown trout rivers and, as they are more aggressive, they have pushed out the native species from their ecological niche. Our true wild brown trout is now regarded as an endangered species as more and more of their rivers fall victim to the twin evils of abstraction and pollution.

Brown trout are much slower-growing than rainbows, and so are not such an attractive proposition for the fish farmer. Nevertheless, many reared fish are released into rivers, thus destroying the genetic makeup of the native wild strains for ever.

Above: Fly fishing for salmon on the River Tay, Scotland.

Salmon Farms

Salmon have gone from being a poor man's meal in the Middle Ages to a rich man's dish in the twentieth century. However, today's modern salmon-farming techniques have recently introduced it onto the supermarket shelves, where it is now cheaper to buy than cod.

Yet, once again, there has been an environmental price to pay as chemicals used to kill sea lice on caged salmon have leached into the coastal waters and driven away the native sea trout.

The Atlantic salmon is becoming rarer in the wild, despite the removal of many commercial estuary nets. Anglers are now asked to return fish to the river, as is common practice in North America.

In past centuries, the salmon ran many of the larger rivers in Britain, like the Trent and the Thames, before pollution at their mouths stopped them entering these waters. Even today, odd fish still make their way upstream on a flood tide, while hundreds of thousands of pounds have been spent on a scheme to try to restore a salmon run to the Thames. Whether it will ever be truly successful must depend on summer flows and dissolved oxygen levels.

In the meantime, those salmon anglers who can afford it now travel to the virgin rivers of northern Russia for their sport, for this is a countrywhere dozens of Atlantic salmon can still be caught on a fly in a day.

Above: A specimen sea trout from the Baltic, caught on a spinner.

DEEP-LIVING CHAR

The Arctic char lives so deep in its glacial lake home that it is rarely seen by anglers. Nevertheless, increased use of power boating and other developments in its natural Lake District home present a threat. This is another fish that is now being farmed commercially.

Sharing its glacial home are the rare whitefish – vendace, powan, skelly and gwyniad which are all indigenous to certain lakes and lochs. These small-mouthed *salmonids* are now protected by law.

Vanishing Sea Trout

The story of the enigmatic sea trout is much the same with runs totally disappearing on some rivers in Scotland, Wales and Ireland. However, other rivers in places like South Wales have enjoyed a sea-trout revival as traditional heavy industries and coal mines have shut down and so stopped polluting the streams.

Possibly the world's best sea-trout fishing is now to be found in the almost tideless waters of the Baltic Sea off Sweden and Denmark. Here double-figure fish are common as they enjoy feasting on the Baltic herring, a prey fish that has swollen in numbers due to the overfishing of their natural predators, the cod.

ATLANTIC SALMON *(Salmo salar)*

- **IDENTIFICATION:** Bright silver with a few dark spots when fresh run from the sea. As they ripen for spawning, the silver fades to a bronze-pink. Cock fish acquire a reddish-brown mottling and a large kype (hooked lower jaw). Hen fish acquire a purplish sheen.
- **SIZE:** Grilse (young salmon returning to fresh water after one winter in the sea) average 6 to 7lb (2.72-3.18kg). 'Springers' returning after two or more winters at sea can weigh up to 30lb (13.6kg) or more.
- **BRITISH RECORD:** 64lb (29.03kg), River Tay, Scotland, 1922.
- **HABITAT:** Clean, cold-temperate and Arctic rivers of northern hemisphere.
- **DISTRIBUTION:** Fast-flowing rivers in Scotland, Wales, Ireland, Northern England and the West Country. But Hampshire's River Test and Avon enjoy a small, but significant, run of big fish.
- **BEST FLIES:** Blue Charm, Garry Dog, Green Highlander, General Practitioner, Thunder & Lightning.
- **SEASON:** February–November (varies on each river system).

SALMON ARE widely regarded as the 'king' of fish, thanks to their dramatic lifestyle as they battle against all the odds that nature and man can throw at them. Their fighting abilities are matched only by their looks and reputation as a table fish. The commercial farming of salmon has led to less pressure on wild stocks, but they are still under threat from pollution, abstraction, disease and overfishing. All members of the Salmonidae family have a small, fleshy adipose fin between the dorsal and the tail.

Habits

Salmon spawn in freshwater, usually in the feeder streams or headwaters of fast-flowing, cool rivers, in late autumn and winter. The hen fish selects an area of gravel to cut her redd (nest), into which she releases her eggs. These are then fertilized by the cock fish, and the redd is then covered to prevent predation by small trout.

Below: Fly fishing for salmon on the River Spey, Scotland.

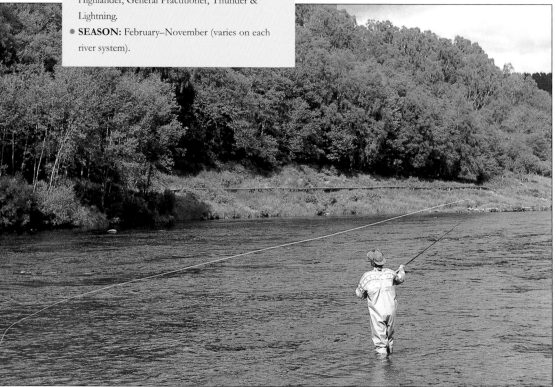

TOP TIP

Salmon fishing can cost you an arm and a leg – or very little. Before booking an expensive beat for a week, why not try an association water first? There are plenty of salmon bargains to be had in Wales, the North-West and the West Country. You will have to share the bank with other anglers, and be prepared to fish at a moment's notice when a sudden spate brings in the fish.

Left: No wonder that salmon are regarded as the 'king' of fish. This fly-caught specimen displays the bright silver flanks of a fish fresh from the sea. Right: General Practitioner is a useful salmon fly.

After spawning, the hen fish (kelt) drops downstream into quieter, deeper water to recover. Some kelts may eventually make it back to the sea, and return again to spawn the following summer. Few cock fish, however, survive.

The salmon eggs hatch into alevin (a stage of development in which they feed from their external yolk sacs) in spring, remaining in the redd for several weeks before emerging as fry. Only around ten percent of the fry may make it to the parr stage.

After two to three years in the river, the baby salmon have grown into smolts measuring six to eight inches (15-20cm) in length, and are ready to drop downstream to saltwater. This usually takes place in spring.

Once in the sea, the rich food supply ensures rapid growth. Shrimps, prawns, squid, sprats and sandeel put on the weight. Some salmon may swim as far as Greenland in a three-year odyssey of heroic proportions before responding to the urge to return to the river of their birth.

Tactics

Salmon returning from the sea do not feed in freshwater, a fact which puzzles many anglers who regularly catch them on fly, bait and spinner. Memory, aggression, inquisitiveness are all put forward as possible reasons for salmon taking a fly or bait. But the truth is that no-one knows for certain.

The great spring runs on the famous Scottish rivers are now a thing of the past, with fresh fish moving into the rivers from late May onwards whenever a suitable spate occurs.

If the water is deep, high and coloured, then the fly angler will need to use a heavy brass tube fly or Waddington to reach the bottom where the salmon will be lying. The fly is cast and allowed to swing round in the current with the angler following it down the pool. Double-handed salmon rods can reach 18ft (5.48m).

As the water clears and drops in level, the salmon angler reduces his fly size accordingly. In low, warm water in summer, a size 10 Stoat's Tail will replace the size 4 and 6s of spring.

Above: Ally's Shrimp is a popular double-hook fly.

SEA TROUT *(Salmo trutta)*

- **IDENTIFICATION:** A sea trout fresh in the river from the sea is a bright bar of silver, speckled with a few black spots. You can tell it from a grilse (young salmon) by the square tail (a salmon's tail is forked) and the long jaw that extends behind the eye. As with the salmon, they darken up the longer they stay in freshwater, and a large gravid (pregnant) fish may be difficult to tell apart from a similar-sized salmon in spawning colours.
- **SIZE:** Small shoal sea trout (also known as peal, finnock or herling) will average around a pound (0.45kg) in weight. But depending on the time spent at sea, they can return from 3lb (1.36kg) up to double figures.
- **BRITISH RECORD:** 28lb 5oz 4dr (12.85kg), River Test, Hampshire, 1992.
- **HABITAT:** Fast-flowing rivers with access to the sea. They are also found in some Scottish lochs and Irish loughs.
- **DISTRIBUTION:** Found right around the British and Irish coastlines. They will run up any river provided it has clear, clean tributary streams suitable for spawning. Wales, Scotland, the West Country and western Ireland are its traditional strongholds.
- **BEST FLIES:** Peter Ross, Alexandra, Red Stuart, Medicine, Bloody Butcher, Blackie, Loch Ordie.
- **SEASON:** March to October.

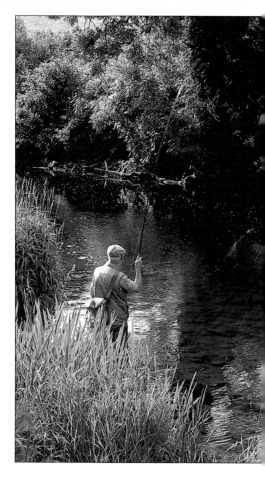

Above: Casting for daytime sea trout on River Teifi, Wales. Many anglers prefer to target sea trout after dark, when the better fish start to move and feed. A warm night without any moon is best.

FEW FISH fire the flyfisherman's imagination more than the mysterious sea trout. One day the pools are empty. The next night, the sea trout have arrived and are leaping. An enigmatic fish with a mind of its own, sea trout inspire a fanaticism among their followers that can border on the obsessive. Recent years have been difficult for the sea trout with runs declining badly in some areas. Chemicals used in fish farming have been blamed. However, other rivers where water quality has improved have seen sea trout runs returning after an absence of years.

Habits

Genetically, sea and brown trout are the same species. In fact, it could be argued that all trout are sea trout by ancestry because our rivers and lakes were originally colonized by trout from the sea.

Like the salmon, Atlantic sea trout spawn in early winter with the female cutting her redd (nest) in the clean gravel of a well-oxygenated feeder stream. The cock fish then fertilizes the eggs, which are covered over by the hen fish.

The adult fish, now known as kelts, move downstream into deeper water to rest before heading back to sea. Survival rates for sea trout kelts are generally higher than for salmon, where 90 percent of cock fish can perish.

For the first two to three years of their lives, the young sea trout are identical to young brown trout. But the genetic difference 'kicks in' as they grow from parr to smolt and turn silver as they head downstream for the sea in spring. More importantly, they develop the physiology to cope with saltwater.

Where they go in the sea is not completely understood. But they have been found in the North Sea feeding on sprats and sandeels, although many are thought to stay in the vicinity of their home estuary.

Many young fish (herling) return to their native river after just a few months at sea, but return again to the sea just as quickly. And the longer they remain in saltwater, the larger they grow. One 11lb (5kg) Scottish fish had been at sea for seven years.

Tactics

After two or more years in saltwater, the urge to reproduce drives the sea trout back to the river of its birth. Low water is no obstacle to the sea trout, which can splash upstream from pool to pool. Unlike the salmon, sea trout feed to some degree in fresh water. Herling will readily attack a fly and need protecting from greedy anglers.

However, to catch the larger fish demands a nocturnal approach as the better fish start to move only at the onset of dusk, especially in conditions of low, clear water. The flyfisherman needs to be in position well before dark to

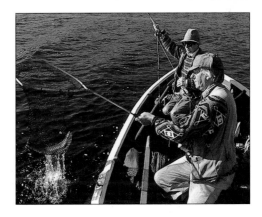

TOP TIP
Try a floating, surface-disturbance pattern fly on a warm night. Let it swing round in the current on a floating line, and then strip it back quickly.

reconnoitre the pool. A warm night without any moon is usually considered best.

Sea trout are easily scared, and noise and light must be kept to a minimum. Those devotees of the sport say sea-trout fishing at night is the best of all.

Above: Fishing for sea trout on Loch Hope, Sutherland.

Below: A large fly-caught sea trout from River Towy, Wales.

WILD BROWN TROUT *(Salmo trutta)*

- **IDENTIFICATION:** Wide variation in the markings which can range from a metallic silver body with dark spots, to a golden yellow with vivid red spots. Unlike the rainbow trout, there are no spots on the tail fin. There are many localized populations that have developed their own characteristic markings over thousands of years. The most well-known example is Ulster's Lough Melvin with its distinctive Gillaroo, Sonaghan and Ferox strains of brown trout.
- **SIZE:** Average 6oz-1lb 8oz (170g-0.8kg)
- **BRITISH RECORD:** 25lb 6oz (11.51kg), Loch Awe, Scotland, 1996.
- **HABITAT:** Fast-flowing clear rivers, natural upland lakes and lochs.
- **DISTRIBUTION:** South-west and northern England, Wales, Scotland, Ireland. Chalk streams in southern England.
- **BEST FLIES:** Zulu, Black Pennell, Butcher, Bibio, Olive Bumble, Mallard & Claret, Connemara Black (lakes); Adams, Beacon Beige, Kite's Imperial, March Brown, Wickham's Fancy, Partridge & Orange, Grey Wulff, Pheasant Tail Nymph (rivers).
- **SEASON:** 1 April-30 September. (15 March-17 October, Wales)

THE BROWN TROUT is indigenous to Europe, north-west Asia and even North Africa, and is the fish that started the whole culture of fly fishing. In the days of the British Empire, when much of the world's map was coloured red, fly-fishing colonialists successfully transported the fertilized eggs of our native brown trout to suitable rivers around the globe. Eggs from the River Itchen in Hampshire were taken to Tasmania in 1864. These were later used to stock Australian and New Zealand waters, which now offer some of the very best brown-trout fishing in the world.

Further stockings were to follow in India, South and East Africa, Argentina, Chile and finally North America, where our trout are still known as German browns.

Sadly, the genuine wild brown trout is fast becoming an endangered species in England and Wales. This is due to abstraction of rivers, urban development, pollution, acid rain and the mixing of strains with stocked fish. The Wild Trout Society has been set up to help safeguard the few remaining pockets of genetically pure wild browns.

The picture is much healthier in Scotland and the west of Ireland where the large lochs still support good heads of wild fish.

Habits

Brown trout require a good flow of healthy oxygenated water to breed. The fertilized eggs which are laid in the gravel bed of a river or lake feeder stream in early winter hatch out after 30 days or more as *alevins*. Once they have used up the food from the yolk sac, they first become known as *fry*, and then *parr* with characteristic finger markings down the sides. All trout have the genetic potential to migrate to the sea, and at this early stage it is impossible to distinguish between the parr of brown and sea trout. Breeding takes place any time after three years.

Size can vary greatly, depending on the natural food available. For example, a four-year-old trout on a moorland stream may weigh only 4oz (113g). By contrast, a trout of similar age from a food-rich chalkstream may weigh 1.5lb (0.68kg). Brown trout are much slower growing than rainbows, but they can reach double-figure weights in the wild in ten years or so if they switch from an insect to a small-fish diet .

Above: Upper River Wharfe in Yorkshire is a famous trout stream. Right: Wild brown trout show an amazing variety of colours and spots, depending on the water from which they come.

FAMOUS WILD BROWN TROUT RIVERS
Usk, Wales; Tweed, Scotland; Itchen, Hampshire; Dove, Derbyshire; Frome, Dorset.

FAMOUS WILD BROWN TROUT LAKES
Windermere, Loch Garry, Loch Ness, Loch Harray, Loch Awe, Loch Quoich, Lough Corrib, Lough Mask, Lough Conn.

SPITTING FEATHERS
Wild brownies can take your fly and spit it out again in a fraction of a second. So complete concentration is required on the part of the fisherman. Always put the bushiest fly on the top dropper and dibble it in the water for a few seconds before lifting out to recast.

Above: Taking a wild brown trout on the drift in a Scottish loch.

Tactics

On chalkstreams, the wild brown trout can be very cautious and demand an exact imitation of the natural flies that are hatching. However, at other times, such as the Mayfly weeks, it will throw caution to the wind and greedily grab the offered pattern. Generally early morning and late evening offer the best chance of success.

In its natural habitat of upland lakes and lochs, it is an opportunistic feeder and will hunt the surface for wind-blown flies and beetles. This is why dark flies work so well, particularly when moved quickly.

On upland rivers, the traditional North Country spider patterns that represent a whole host of underwater insects are usually favoured.

CULTIVATED BROWN TROUT

- **IDENTIFICATION:** A mixture of colours and shapes ranging from highly-marked deep-bodied small-water fish, to silver grown-on reservoir fish.
- **SIZE:** 2-10lb (0.9-4.5kg)
- **BRITISH RECORD:** 28lb 1oz (12.73kg), Dever Springs, Hampshire, 1995.
- **HABITAT:** Small clear stillwaters, large gravel pits, lowland reservoirs.
- **DISTRIBUTION:** Anywhere in the UK.
- **BEST FLIES:** Sweeney Todd, Ace of Spades, Goldie, Muddler Minnow, Appetizer, Cat's Whisker, Viva, Floating Fry, Olive Dog Nobbler, Lead Bug, When All Else Fails, Gold and Silver Tube.
- **SEASON:** 1 April-31 October.

BROWN trout are more difficult to rear artificially than rainbow trout, and also more expensive. But that has not stopped fish farmers and fisheries from growing some absolute monsters. There is even talk of a potential 40-pounder (18kg), a weight that would be impossible to achieve in the wild.

Brown trout can be stocked into a stillwater of virtually any size. And although they stand no chance of breeding, they can live for a number of years – often without ever being caught.

Reservoirs tend to stock brown trout anything from a pound up to three pounds (0.5-1.4kg). Initially, they are the

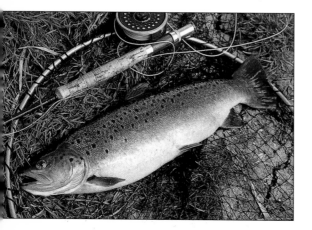

Above: The plump body of a stocked small-water brown trout.

easiest fish in the reservoir to catch as they hang around the margins in shoals. But they gradually wise up and turn on to natural food. As they do so, they actually change shape and colour. And the longer they stay uncaught in the reservoir, the more silver and sleek they become.

Given the rich food supply of small coarse fish available, they can attain astounding weights. Last year saw a 19-pound (8.6kg) brown trout caught from Grafham, Cambridgeshire, and a 20-pounder (9kg) taken from Bewl, Kent. Both took deadbaits meant for pike. Flyfishermen have recorded unofficial records of 18lb 13.5oz (8.5kg) from Wentwood Reservoir, Gwent, in 1990 and 17lb 2oz (7.8kg) from Rutland Water, Leicestershire, in 1994.

In some small waters, brown trout are actually stocked at similar weights for anglers to catch. These has been much criticism of these 'instant records' but the practice shows no sign of diminishing. Many of the largest browns have been at liberty for only a few hours before capture.

Habits

Brown trout in the wild are naturally territorial, and they behave in similar fashion when stocked in small waters. They will often patrol the margins of the same small corner of a lake, making them an easy target for observant anglers. However, they do learn quickly and if they escape capture on the morning they are stocked, it may be weeks or even months before they are finally taken. If they are at liberty for some time, they will eventually lose weight.

Below left: This beautiful grown-on brown trout was taken from Roadford Lake, Cornwall.

FAMOUS STOCKED BROWN TROUT WATERS

Loch Leven, Scotland; Blagdon Water, Somerset; Rutland Water, Leicestershire; Carsington Water, Derbyshire; Roadford Lake, Cornwall; Dever Springs, Hampshire; Chalk Springs, Sussex; River Test, Hampshire.

Right: Carsington Water in Derbyshire is run as a brown trout-only fishery. Cultivated brownies can grow to huge sizes.

On a reservoir or large gravel pit, they are easy to catch for a week or so. Then they simply disappear into the depths, reappearing only in the autumn to feed around the margins on fry or vainly attempt to spawn. In the future, fish farmers may stock with triploid (sexless) browns which would ensure their condition year round and do away with the need for any close season on stocked stillwaters.

Tactics

On small clear stillwaters, the only way to take a brown trout is by stalking it and dropping a leaded fly or nymph close to its head. You need to appeal to the trout's natural aggression, rather than its feeding instinct, to persuade it to take the fly. The experienced angler can tell a brown trout from a rainbow underwater and target a particular fish.

On reservoirs or larger stocked waters, spring and autumn are really the only times when you can set your

FINDING THE BEST LOCATION FOR BROWN TROUT

When boat fishing for brown trout on a reservoir, always look for a gravel bed or underwater raised island. The brown trout will not be too far away.

Above: This specimen predatory Rutland Water brownie fell to a tinsel tube fly fished deep in the water.

stall out for browns only. Many big fish are caught by bank anglers in the opening weeks of April on lures as the fish feed up after winter.

In autumn comes the other opportunity when the browns swim right into the shallows to chase small fish for food. However, they can be difficult and will not simply take any fly cast at them. A small Floating Fry fished near weedbeds or a Minkie fished just under the surface at first light will work, as will a tube fly up to five inches (12.7cm) long fished round in an arc behind a fast-drifting boat.

RAINBOW TROUT *(Oncorhynchus mykiss)*

- **IDENTIFICATION:** Bottle-green back with violet-pink band running along the side from eye to tail. The small dark spots are carried through to the tail fin.
- **SIZE:** Varies widely depending on size stocked. Average is 1lb 4oz (0.57kg), going up to 20lb (9kg)plus.
- **BRITISH RECORD:** 36lb 14oz 8dr (16.74kg), Dever Springs, Hampshire, 1995.
- **RESIDENT RECORD:** 18lb 9oz (8.42kg), Hanningfield Reservoir, Essex, 1995.
- **HABITAT:** Very adaptable. Can be found in lakes, ponds and rivers. Breeds wild in Derbyshire Wye.
- **DISTRIBUTION:** Anywhere in the UK, but rare in northern Scotland.
- **BEST FLIES:** On its day, anything will work. Montana, Damsel Nymph, Black Buzzer, Claret Hopper, Orange Tadpole, Peach Doll, Gold Ribbed Hare's Ear, and Booby Nymph are classics.
- **SEASON:** All year

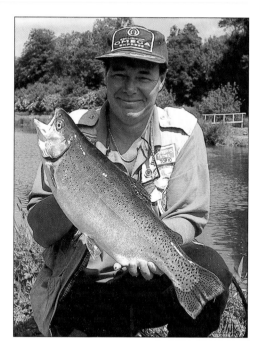

THE FIGHTING rainbow trout is a native of North America, specifically the west coast rivers from California right up to Alaska. Because it is an easy fish to raise in hatcheries and is tolerant of a wide range of water types and temperatures, the rainbow trout has been stocked in rivers and lakes around the world including New Zealand, Australia and South America.

In Britain, the rainbow trout is thought of purely as a stillwater fish. It is not popular in rivers as its aggressive feeding behaviour will supplant the native brown trout.

It only rarely breeds in the wild in Britain, the Derbyshire Wye being the most famous example. For this reason, the fish enjoys no close-season protection. However, the fish can run into spawning condition in early winter with cock fish becoming black and unsightly. Consequently, fisheries tend to stock hen fish only or triploid (sexless) rainbows.

There are many pure strains of rainbow trout in the wild – Shasta, Kamloops and Golden are just three examples. But these strains have now become so mixed in the fish hatcheries that it is impossible to identify a rainbow's pedigree.

A rainbow trout that is stocked into a large water like a reservoir or gravel pit will slowly change shape and colour over the months as it reverts to natural feeding. Much of the spotting will disappear with the fish developing a more natural silver colour. The fins will also develop as the fish has more room to move and further to swim.

These trout are known by anglers as 'resident' or 'overwintered' fish, and are highly prized both for their appearance and their fighting ability.

They contrast with the giant rainbows stocked into many small waters. These bloated monsters, reared on a super-rich diet of pellets, can never sustain their weight in such small waters and need to be caught quickly if they are not to lose condition. Usually they are caught, often on the very day they were stocked.

Habits

The rainbow is a greedy, competitive feeder which makes it so suitable for stocking into fisheries. However, they soon learn what flies to avoid and the longer they are in the water, the more difficult they become to catch. On waters where catch-and-release is allowed, the resident rainbows become vary wary indeed, demanding the finest lines and smallest flies.

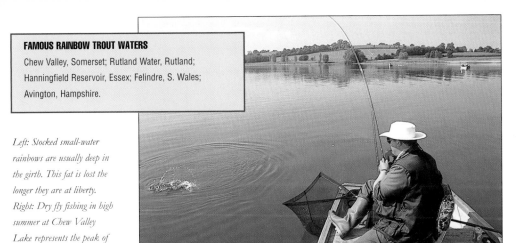

FAMOUS RAINBOW TROUT WATERS

Chew Valley, Somerset; Rutland Water, Rutland;
Hanningfield Reservoir, Essex; Felindre, S. Wales;
Avington, Hampshire.

Left: Stocked small-water rainbows are usually deep in the girth. This fat is lost the longer they are at liberty. Right: Dry fly fishing in high summer at Chew Valley Lake represents the peak of rainbow trout sport.

They are much faster growing than brown trout, reaching sexual maturity at the end of their second year. But in the wild they rarely live for more than four or five years. A wild four-year-old rainbow may be 6lb (2.7kg). In a fish farm, that same fish may reach 20lb (9kg). In reservoirs, a resident rainbow may survive long enough to reach double figures. But three to five pounds (1.4-2.3kg) is the usual weight.

Like all trout, rainbows can become preoccupied with a particular food form. But they are catholic feeders and will take whatever is most abundant. On reservoirs this is often daphnia, but they will also eat snails, midge, nymphs and fry.

Tactics

Freshly stocked fish on a small water often require little skill to catch, taking any quickly pulled fly with gusto. However, it is a different story on a big water where they have learned to feed naturally. Here the angler may have to try every fly in the box, from small nymphs on a floating line to a lure on a fast sinker.

Left: A beautiful example of a grown-on rainbow trout caught from a reservoir.

Above: Catch-and-release is permitted on some rainbow trout waters.

EARLY BIRD

On a small water, try to be the first on the bank as the freshly stocked fish will be the easiest to catch. On a large water, you must find the fish first either by asking local fishermen or looking for rising fish.

BROOK TROUT *(Salvelinus fontinalis)*

- **IDENTIFICATION:** The back is a striking greyish-green with distinctive mottling (vermiculations) forming a marbled pattern. Cream to greenish-yellow spots along its flanks mix with red and blue ones. The white belly is tinged with orange that darkens to almost red at spawning time, while the anal, pelvic and pectoral fins are edged with white, backed by a narrow black strip.
- **SIZE:** Average 1lb 8oz to 4lb (0.68-1.8kg).
- **BRITISH RECORD:** 5lb 13oz 8dr (2.65kg), Avington, Hampshire 1981.
- **HABITAT:** Cool, clear, clean water. Thrives in acidic moorland lakes and reservoirs.
- **DISTRIBUTION:** Natural to North America. Now stocked artificially in stillwater lakes and reservoirs across the UK.
- **BEST FLIES:** Any brightly-coloured lure.
- **SEASON:** All year.

TOP TIP

Brook trout are much more aggressive than rainbows and will often attack a bright lure with a vengeance, even in the coldest weather.

THERE ARE few more beautiful fish to catch than members of the char family. A native of cold water regions, these spectacularly coloured game fish are sought around the world in the temperate and Arctic regions.

The char most familiar to British fly anglers is the American brook trout, a native of eastern North America which has been bred and stocked around the world. They are now found in Europe, Asia, New Zealand, South America and South Africa.

The larger brook trout are usually stocked on the small, clear fisheries where they can be successfully stalked. The white edges to their belly fins can be seen underwater, helping the angler to identify the quarry before he or she even casts.

Brookies can often be much easier to catch than the more-wily rainbow or brownie, with a habit of attacking the fly avidly. They also have a tendency to shoal up, and good numbers of fish can be taken shortly after stocking.

Being a native of cold, northern waters, brook trout do well in the more acidic moorland lakes and reservoirs of the west and north of Britain, where food can be in short supply. Self-sustaining populations in west coast Scottish hill lochs have been extensively studied, and were found to be very catholic in their food choice, happily consuming tadpoles and small frogs. They can put on weight and rise freely on waters where other trout may struggle to thrive. Hence their popularity with fishery owners in Wales and Scotland.

Fish farmers like to experiment with brook trout, crossing them with brown trout to produce the spectacularly marked tiger trout. These are now rarer than used to be the case, but every season sees some caught.

Above: A fine American brook trout from Chalk Springs, Sussex.

ARCTIC CHAR *(Salvelinus alpinus)*

- **IDENTIFICATION:** Dark olive-green on the back with mottled cream markings on the flanks. At spawning time, the bellies are vivid fireball red and orange with brilliant white leading edges to the belly fins.
- **SIZE:** Average 12oz to 1lb 4oz (0.34-0.57kg). But much larger fish are now being taken in Scotland.
- **BRITISH RECORD:** 8lb 8dr (3.64kg), Loch Arkaig, Inverness, 1992.
- **HABITAT:** Deep, clear, glacial lakes. They have been recorded as deep as 400ft (120m).
- **DISTRIBUTION:** Throughout Arctic regions. In the British Isles they are restricted to Snowdonia, the Lake District and Scottish Highland lochs.
- **BEST FLIES:** Traditional wets like Butcher for small fish; large stillwater fish are usually caught deep, on trolled plugs. Use salmon flies with red and gold for river-running char.
- **SEASON:** March–October

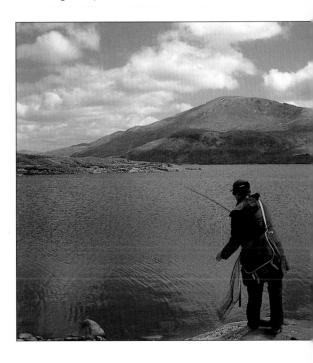

Above: A deep Highland loch is the natural home of the char.

TOP TIP

Char are not easy to catch on the fly. The best time is a calm evening or night when they dimple the surface after small flies.

THE WILD relation of the brook trout in the British Isles is the legendary Arctic char. Relict populations exist in the deep, glacial lakes of North Wales, Cumbria and Scotland, such as Windermere and Loch Rannoch. In the past, these fish were rarely caught except by the dedicated professional char fishermen who fish small spinners very deep on specialized tackle. However, Arctic char have now become a popular sport quarry, pursued by specialist char anglers.

For many years, a char of 12 ounces to a pound (340-450g) would have been a good fish from a British lake. However, since the advent of salmon-rearing cages in the Highlands, char weights have taken off, as the fish have learned to feed on the waste fish pellets passing through the cages.

Char in excess of six and seven pounds (2.72-3.18kg) have been taken from Loch Arkaig, including the current 8lb (3.64kg) record. Double-figure char are not out of the question as they grow to more than 20lb (9kg) in Europe and Scandinavia.

Char are now turning up on the wet-fish counters of major supermarkets as fish farmers turn to rearing them artificially, bringing in foreign strains of char. All of the

genus *Salvelinus* can be hybridized artificially to produce some exotic offspring. But it would be a mistake for the genetic integrity of our native char to be lost by cross-breeding.

In the rivers of the high Arctic, char run to sea. It is doubtful whether this still happens in the British Isles, but we can be certain that our resident char stocks are descended from a migratory stock which entered the deglaciated river systems 12,000 years ago. Spawning takes place in the spring on the gravel banks of lakes, or in autumn in rivers and feeder streams.

Their red flesh is extremely tasty, thanks to their varied natural diet of insects and crustaceans. It is common to find eels attacking and eating char caught in a gill net, while ignoring brown trout.

GRAYLING *(Thymallus thymallus)*

- **IDENTIFICATION:** Giant purple-tinged dorsal fin with dark spots, silver flanks with iridescent mauve tinge. Large scales in rows, small adipose fin, underslung mouth.
- **SIZE:** Average 8oz-1lb 4oz (227g-0.6kg). A two-pounder (0.9kg) is a specimen.
- **BRITISH RECORD:** 4lb 3oz (1.9kg), River Frome, Dorset, 1989.
- **HABITAT:** Fast-flowing clear rivers with gravel bottoms.
- **DISTRIBUTION:** Southern England chalk streams; northern and Welsh freestone rivers. None in Ireland.
- **BEST FLIES:** Red Tag, Terry's Terror, Killer Bug, Leaded Shrimp, Snipe & Purple.
- **SEASON:** 16 June-14 March.

Above: A grayling comes to the hand on a southern chalk stream. Note the grayling's large sail-like dorsal fin.

Below: The author, Chris Dawn, with a fine grayling caught on a dry mayfly from the upper Hampshire Avon.

THERE ARE few more handsome fish than the grayling, which occurs in natural fast-flowing rivers right across Britain and Northern Europe, with the larger Arctic grayling also to be found in Lapland, Siberia and Northern Canada.

Once regarded as unwanted vermin on British trout streams, the grayling is now accepted as a worthwhile

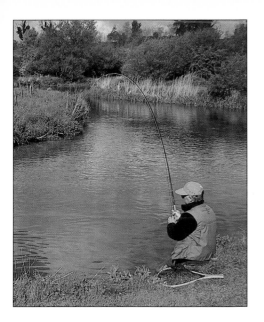

quarry in its own right. Southern chalk streams, where grayling were once electrofished and removed, now open their exclusive doors in winter for the growing band of grayling anglers. There is even a Grayling Society, which organizes competitions and days out for its members.

Although technically a game fish because of its adipose fin, the grayling breeds in spring and so enjoys the same legal protection on rivers as coarse fish. However, they will often take the fly right through the year, although autumn and early winter are the best times to seek the grayling. When the water is cold, the grayling is at its fittest.

Habits

At spawning time in May or early June, the cock grayling wraps its large dorsal fin over the back of the hen, stimulating her to drop her eggs onto the gravel. This is in sharp contrast to trout who bury their eggs.

Due to their slim, muscular body shape, grayling are happy to lie in the fastest water – often in large shoals. Shallow water is often favoured, although they do prefer some weed cover close by. The larger, more solitary, fish will often be found lurking in a deeper pool or behind a midstream boulder.

Grayling are free-rising fish and are not easily put off by clumsy casting. But the smaller fish can be difficult to hook as they rise almost vertically from the bottom to suck in the fly, and then return straight to their lie on the bottom.

FAMOUS GRAYLING RIVERS

Dee, Wales; Ure, Yorkshire; Test, Hampshire; Wye, Derbyshire; Wylye, Wiltshire.

Left: Grayling will rise repeatedly to a dry fly from their lie on gravel shallows. Shoals of these handsome fish are often very dense and they appear reluctant to move away from their chosen swim. Many fish can, therefore, be taken from the same shoal.

Tactics

Dry fly is the classic way to take grayling, and can work even on the coldest of days. Look for a shallow run, particularly below a weir or gravel bar, and fish your dry fly upstream. If you miss a rise, the chances are that the fish will come to it again on the following cast. Always give the grayling enough time to turn down with the fly.

The other way to take grayling is to fish a leaded fly, like a Sawyer's Killer Bug or a Goldhead Hare's Ear, either cast upstream or allowed to swing down and across the current. Watch the leader for any quick darts as the grayling sucks in the fly. Or use a strike indicator to tell you when the grayling has taken.

Grayling have a habit of lying close together, so it is possible to take fish after fish from the same shoal. In fact small grayling can become a nuisance in their suicidal efforts to suck in your fly. To find the better-sized fish, you will probably need to use a heavily leaded nymph that gets down in the current to the deeper holes. Takes can be quite vicious and you can be broken on a light leader if you are fishing straight downstream.

Alternatively, try swinging a team of Spiders around in the current. If the trout are not feeding, it is odds on that the grayling will be.

In winter on the southern chalk streams, the grayling tend to hole up in big shoals in the slack corners of the deeper carriers. Here they can be almost too easy to catch on small nymphs like the Killer Bug, taking it with the abandon of a maggot!

HANDLE WITH CARE

Despite their fighting abilities, grayling are sensitive fish and need careful handling if you intend to return them. Always hold them in the current first with head upstream, making sure they are strong enough to swim away before releasing them.

TECHNIQUES

TACKLING UP

WITH SO much fly-fishing tackle available, it is easy to become confused when considering what to buy. As a first step, set yourself a realistic budget – one that you can afford. Then visit a good tackle shop and ask for assistance. Before you go, it is worth looking at the prices in mail order advertisements and catalogues so you have a good idea of what you should be paying for each item of equipment. Most shops should give some discount for cash, particularly if you make a substantial purchase.

Alternatively, you can obtain all of the goods by mail order, but you should really have a cast with the rod first to make sure it suits you before you buy. Some mail order companies are only too pleased for you to visit their showrooms to try a rod out before you spend any money. And they often offer attractive deals on rods that are suitable for beginners.

What Rod?

Your first rod should be a 9ft 6in (2.9m) #7/8 medium action. If, however, you plan to start boat fishing straight away as well, then go a ten footer (3.05m). This type of rod should cost somewhere between £80 and £150. Beware of buying a rod that is too cheap. As with everything else in life, you get what you pay for.

Most modern fly rods are well made, but beware of very light rods offered at low cost. These may cast extremely well, but the walls of the glass-fibre blank are thin and liable to shatter if struck with a heavy fly, or if the rod falls awkwardly.

Whatever you do, avoid buying a cheap sloppy rod with no backbone. You will just get into bad casting habits that will be difficult to kick later.

Another point worth considering is the fit of the rod handle in your hand. Depending upon the size of your hand, some handles may feel too thin while others will feel too thick. Again, you will only be able to determine the correct handle by trying the rod before you buy.

Other Tackle

You need spend no more than £20 to £30 on your first reel. Until you become more experienced, the reel will be used only for line storage. But you will need a spare spool to hold an extra line.

Left: The modern flyfisher is able to select neoprene waders and a shortie wading jacket to complete his choice of tackle.

Right: Make sure that you put your fly reel on the rod handle the correct way round, so that the line comes off the front of the spool.

TOP TIP

You may prefer to change your reel from right-hand to left-hand wind. On many fly reels you can achieve this by reversing the central cog.

Below: A black and green Tadpole pattern will catch fish at any water.

As far as fly lines are concerned, there are dozens on the market. But for a start you will need just a floater and a medium sinker. Again, expect to pay around £20 for each reasonable quality line. Make sure it feels slick to the touch.

You will need some 82ft (25m) spools of leader material in, say, 5lb and 7lb (2.27kg and 3.18kg) – always choose the clear line. In addition you will require a small mixed box of lures and nymphs, sizes 12 to 8, and that all-important landing net. Polarizing glasses and a brimmed hat are essential protective measures for your eyes, while a fishing waistcoat with its many pockets does away with the necessity for a bag.

First Steps

Assuming your rod is two piece, simply slide the sections together making sure that the rings all align in a straight line. Then screw your reel onto the bottom of the handle (just occasionally they don't fit, so check before you buy), making sure that the line comes off the top of the reel from the front and not the back. There may be a line guard fitted. It is a common fault to see beginners put their reels on upside down.

Thread the line carefully through the rod rings, making sure not to miss one. If you do, you will just have to start again. When you reach the top ring, make sure that you pull off several yards of line. If you do not, the weight of the line will simply make it fall back through the rings and you will have to start again.

Tie on a leader of 12 feet (3.7m) and attach the chosen fly, and you are ready to start fishing.

LEARNING TO CAST

LEARNING TO cast a fly is not easy at first. As with learning to drive a car, some people pick it up straightaway, while others take weeks to achieve an acceptable level of skill. But, like riding a bicycle, once you have learned to cast a fly, you will never forget how to.

However, it is all too easy to get into bad casting habits. So the best advice is to take professional casting lessons. Simply visit your local trout fishery and ask the manager if he gives lessons. Or buy one of the game-fishing magazines and look through the classified advertisements for a game-fishing instructor in your area.

You can start off by practising on a field or your garden lawn. Tie a small piece of wool to the end of the leader in place of a fly, and make sure there is nothing to snag it on behind you.

Basic Overhead Cast

This cast is the basic foundation of all other casts. It involves lifting the line off the water, sweeping it up and behind you to load the rod, and then casting it forwards.

Aim to keep your wrist straight and move your arm only from the elbow. If you 'break' that wrist by letting it bend over on the back cast, the line will drop low behind you and fail to come forward, or may even catch the grass.

Grip the handle so that your thumb is upright and supporting the rod. Assuming that the line is already on the water, lift the rod smoothly using your forearm to pull the line off the surface. As the rod flexes backwards, the line will accelerate upwards and backwards. But do not take the rod too far back. Stop it at about the 'one o'clock' position, and let the tip do the rest of the work.

Also beware of letting your arm stray out to the side too much, otherwise you will end up throwing the line rather than casting it. Ideally, the reel should be in line with your eye at the end of the lift.

Below: The loop of line on a forward cast. The objective is to achieve a parallel line with narrow loops. Give the loop time to straighten out and extend before dropping onto the water.
Right: Shooting the line to gain extra casting distance.

When the line has extended straight out behind you, you can then start to bring the rod forward again. It may help if you glance behind to check that the line has straightened properly before starting the forward cast.

If you start the forward cast too early, you will simply crack the line like a lion-tamer's whip. This is why beginners lose so many flies. However, if you leave it too long, the line will simply lose its momentum and drop to the ground behind you. Instructors encourage their casting pupils to adopt a tapping movement with their wrist to transfer the power of the back cast to the forward cast.

The objective is to cast a parallel line with narrow loops, not one with untidy wide loops that drop behind you, or even hit you on the head as you come forward.

When the line comes forward, try to aim it about three feet (1m) above the water. Give the loop time to straighten out and extend before dropping onto the water. Try to ensure that the tapping movement and the follow-through (achieved by lowering the rod) is done in one continuous action.

You want the line to land as straight as possible, but also with the minimum of splash. So practise first with no more than a few yards of line out through the rings.

Shooting a Line

Once you have mastered the basic overhand cast, you are ready to shoot some line to gain extra distance. Pull off some spools of line and let them fall onto the ground, keeping some spare line in the hand that is not holding the rod.

Maintaining tension on the line, lift it off the water, accelerate the rod to the vertical and stop. Your casting hand can drift back a little, ending up aligned with the top of your head.

Once the line has straightened out behind you – a slight tug will tell you that the rod has fully loaded – bring the rod forward, releasing the spare loop of line that was secured in your other hand. Remember to follow the cast through with the rod for a gentle touchdown.

Once you have got used to releasing that spare line, you can learn to false cast. This consists of moving the rod backwards and forwards between 1.30 and 11 o'clock over your head several times to work increasingly more line into the air. You can then cast further and more accurately to reach a rising fish. This technique also increases the speed at which the line travels, as well as having the benefit of drying out a 'water-logged' fly.

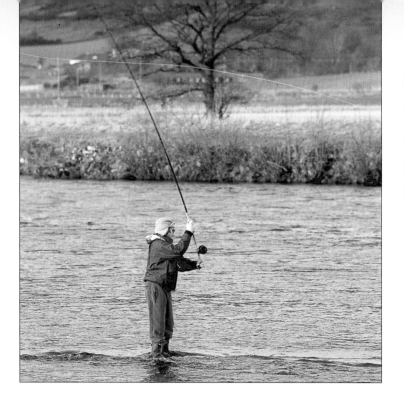

TOP TIP

When netting a trout, always make sure that the net is already submerged in the water so that the fish will not be alarmed at the last minute.

Left: Spey casting on a Scottish salmon river. Opposite top: Hauling the line on the lift. Hauling increases the speed of the line during the cast, thus allowing the angler to reach greater distances. Opposite below: The start of the roll cast.

Hauling

This is a method that allows you to reach great distances by dramatically increasing the speed of the line during the cast. It also helps you to control a line in a strong wind.

In the single haul, the hand that is not holding the rod pulls down, or hauls, on the line during the lift and releases it on the forward cast. In the double haul, the line is pulled down sharply twice – once on the lift when the line is released on the back cast, and again on the forward cast. This extra loading of the rod enables it to perform to its maximum ability.

When shooting large amounts of line from the bank, make sure there are no twigs, weed or pieces of grass attached to it that might hinder the line's progress through the rod rings. Many reservoir anglers use a line tray or basket to hold the loose line for this reason.

Wind can either be the enemy or the friend of the caster. It is obviously easier to cast with a backwind, provided it is not too strong to prevent the line straightening out behind you. But the ability to cast into a headwind, however short a distance, may catch you more fish. A gentle sidewind blowing left to right is often the best compromise for the conventional right-handed angler. For a wind blowing in the opposite direction, it may be necessary to turn and cast over the opposite shoulder, releasing the line on the back cast.

Roll Cast

This is a way of casting the fly without using a backcast. Here the line is lifted off the water to the side of the angler and rolled forward. It is used a lot by river anglers where high banks or trees prevent a conventional cast.

The roll cast starts with the line under tension on the water and the heavy belly of the line behind the angler. The rod is lifted back and up in a semi-circle to pull the line across the water surface.

Then, when the line is looped behind the angler, the rod is brought sharply forward in one flowing movement to roll the line out on the water.

Spey Cast

The roll cast is the basis of the Spey cast, as practised by salmon anglers. The single Spey is normally used by a wading angler when a strong wind is blowing upstream. The double Spey is reserved for when a strong wind is blowing downstream. Either way, the ability to cast off either shoulder is essential.

In the single Spey, the salmon fly rod is raised and swung round upstream to bring line and fly off the water. The line must strike the water after lifting to create the big loop that is used to push the fly back upstream of the rod. The double Spey is a more complex variation where the line is swung back downstream to form the loop.

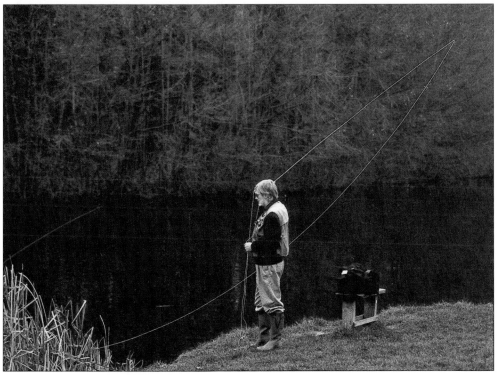

WET-FLY FISHING – RIVERS

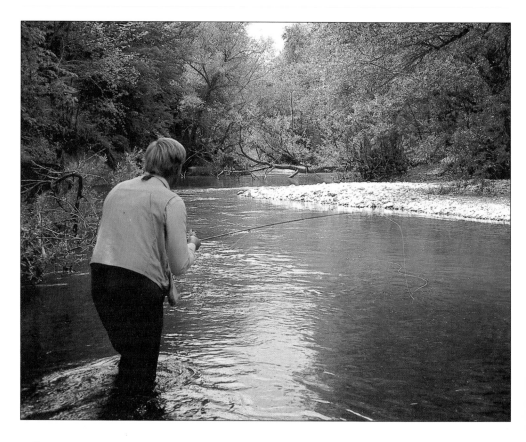

ON NATURAL freestone rivers where nature, rather than man, has created the habitat, there are all types of areas where the trout may be lying. So in the absence of a hatch of fly, the wading angler must work his or her way along the river trying the various locations.

Favoured areas at dawn and dusk are shallows, riffles and runs, while during the day shaded areas under the bank, around fallen trees, and well-oxygenated water below weirs are prime spots to try.

The soft-hackled wet fly is cast out slightly upstream and across the current, then allowed to come round in an arc. Let the line keep pace with the current.

It can pay to add a smaller fly on a dropper above the point fly, which will fish just sub-surface. Takes will often come as the fly swings round at the tail of the pool.

You may see a proper rise form if the fish takes close to the surface, or you may just notice the tip of the line stop or jerk. At any of these signs, strike by raising the rod.

Above: Wet-fly fishing a fast run at the tail of a pool, where the fly is allowed to swing round in the current.

If you miss your fish, move on upstream paying particular attention to the water under the banks and around any large boulders or fallen trees. Try any large eddies or where the current narrows.

River wet flies, with their spider shoulder hackles, are designed for downstream fishing on Britain's northern streams. They are general imitations of nymphs, emerging duns and drowning spinners, with the dressings sometimes dating back hundreds of years. The Bloa series of sparsely dressed flies takes its name from the old word for bluish slatey-grey.

Winged wet flies, like the Coachman and Butcher, seem to work best when fished upstream and jerked back. A larger fly, such as size 12, can be used in spring, dropping down to a size 16 in very low water.

FLOAT TUBING

THIS HIGHLY popular method that originated in the United States is rapidly catching on in the British Isles as more and more stillwaters allow its use. It gives access to areas of bank that otherwise would be quite inaccessible. Float tubing is also now popular in Scotland for fishing remote lochs where no boats are available.

A float tube is basically a lorry tyre inner tube that has been covered in canvas and fitted with webbing for a seat. For safety, there are extra flotation compartments in the back support, while the angler is always encouraged to wear an inflatable lifejacket for added security.

Propulsion is achieved by diving fins worn on the angler's feet, while a pair of neoprene chest waders are essential to stay warm. Always walk backwards when entering the water, making sure that the fins are secured to your ankles with nylon snap catches.

The angler paddles backwards against the wind, using the fins to turn and tread water in order to remain stationary while casting.

A float-tube angler must never enter the lake at the top of the wind as he might then be blown into the centre

> **TOP TIP**
>
> A word of warning... never leave a float tube in a hot car. It will explode!

of the lake, and not have sufficient strength to manage to return to the bank.

A float tube allows the angler to approach the rising trout very closely without alarming them, and is a perfect platform for nymph and dry-fly fishing. But an intermediate line also works well when cast back towards the bank where the shallows suddenly drop away.

A short-handled net is essential, while all the flies and leader material you need can be stowed in the float tube's pockets. It can pay to make sure your fly boxes float.

The float tube may need to be inflated before you get to the fishery at a local garage. Otherwise use a plug-in compressor run from the car.

Below: Float tubing is now being allowed on more and more waters in Britain. It allows the angler to approach the fish closely.

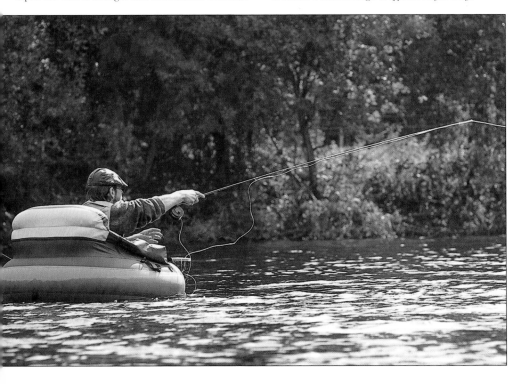

NYMPH FISHING – RIVERS

FOR EVERY trout you see sipping a fly down from the surface, there are another ten feeding unseen on nymphs and other invertebrate food, such as shrimps and caddis. The techniques for catching these deeper-feeding fish on chalkstreams have evolved from methods first made famous by innovative anglers like G.E.M. Skues and later Frank Sawyer.

The Sawyer technique of the 'induced take' is just as deadly today and involves casting far enough ahead of a rising fish so that the nymph sinks to its level, then pulling it up through the water away from the fish at the last moment by lifting the rod. You hope that the trout is induced to grab the fly, by instinct, as it comes past its nose. Watch for a flicker of white as the fish opens its mouth, and then strike.

If you cannot spot a trout hanging or rising in the water, you can still fish the nymph 'dead drift' in a likely area. The fly is cast upstream on a shortish leader and allowed to drift back towards you. The leader must be watched at all times for any sign of a flicker to left or right, and then struck. For either of these methods to be successful, you will need a weighted fly like Sawyer's Pheasant Tail or Killer Bug with their wraps of copper and lead wire.

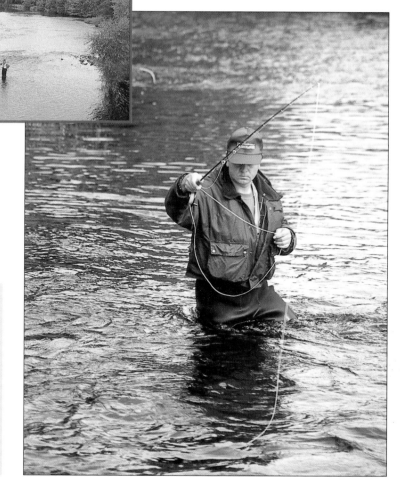

Above and right: Fishing the 'rolled nymph' technique on the Welsh Dee where a heavy point fly is allowed to trundle along the bottom of the river on a dead drift. The rod is held high and the line is kept tight during the drift.

GETTING DOWN TO IT

Some anglers now use lead-injected or weighted braided leaders with gold or silver bead flies to fish deep for grayling in winter. Takes are often registered as a sudden or unusual movement on the line.

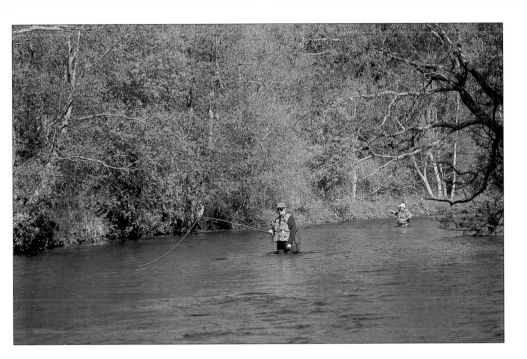

Many of today's river anglers simply pinch a piece of 'float dough' on to the line as a bite indicator and watch that instead of the leader. Takes are shown as quick dips or any sudden halt or movement sideways.

For trout lying deep in sluice pools or in bankside holes, you will need a far-heavier fly, such as a Leaded Shrimp or Goldhead. These are fished on a long leader, cast well upstream and allowed to sink well down to the fish.

On freestone rivers where trout or grayling are often lying behind boulders in the current, these weighted nymphs or shrimps can be cast into the holes and then allowed to swing round in the current in a curve. If the line straightens it could be a trout, so strike.

To ensure the nymph gets down the the fish, you may need to add extra weight like Heavy Metal putty or even split shot to the leader just in front of the fly.

The Rolled Nymph

In recent years, a whole new technique of nymphing has been developed by Eastern European anglers for grayling and trout that are lying deep in the water. They have even developed a special slim, but heavy, fly called the Semtex Nymph for the method.

Known as the rolled nymph, this technique involves slowly wading along the river making short casts with two flies – a heavy nymph on the point and a lighter fly on a

Above: The rivers of the Czech Republic were where the 'rolled nymph' technique was developed.

Below: The slimline Semtex nymphs which are weighted to allow them to be fished deep in the water.

dropper further up the cast. The flies are cast slightly upstream and the rod used to hold the end of the line at the surface while the flies sweep along the river bed in a dead drift.

The rod is held high at the start of the drift to allow the leader and flies to drop straight down in the water, but is lowered as the flies come sweeping past. If no takes are forthcoming, then the rod can be lifted halfway through the cast to sweep the flies off the bottom.

A braided sleeve with two coloured sections (red or orange) of silicone tubing at the end of the line is used to spot takes. Any dip or suspicious movement of the line is struck. It could be the bottom, weed or a fish.

DRY-FLY FISHING – RIVERS

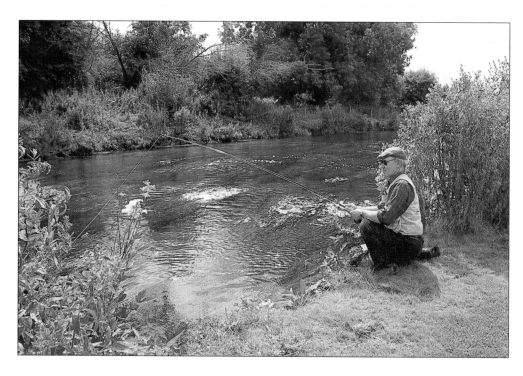

LONG-ACKNOWLEDGED as the purest form of fly fishing, the art of river dry-fly fishing has inspired generations of English and foreign writers, artists, poets and even philosophers to wax lyrical about its pleasures.

On many of the classic chalkstreams in the south of England, such as the Test, Itchen, Kennet and Avon, the rules are strictly upstream dry-fly only. And it is generally frowned upon even to cast speculatively on the water. The angler waits patiently for a rise to begin before he or she starts to fish, and afternoons and evenings are favourite times for duns to hatch.

Rise forms vary widely from hour-to-hour and river-to-river. The experienced river angler will be able to tell how the trout is feeding, and what it is taking, by the way it breaks the surface. The art comes in persuading a particular trout to take your artificial pattern among a host of natural flies.

The classic rise is when a series of concentric rings fan out on the surface as the trout confidently engulfs the fly as it drifts past. Trout do not rise vertically in the water, instead they drift back on the current to intercept the fly. The trout will then return to its station in the stream,

Above: Dry-fly fishing on the Upper Avon in Wiltshire.

usually inbetween weed beds, on a shallow gravel run, under a bridge, overhanging tree or in a hatch pool, to wait for the next free meal.

The challenge comes in first identifying the fly that the trout is taking, whether they are taking duns or spinners, or if they are nymphing sub-surface. River trout can quickly become selective in a mixed hatch of flies, picking out only the one they want and ignoring the rest.

Assuming that you have selected the correct artificial imitation, the next challenge comes in persuading the trout to take it.

Get yourself into a casting position downstream of the fish, but whatever you do, don't cast over the fish. The trout should see the fly first, rather than your line and leader. If the trout does take the fly, do not be in too much of a hurry to strike. Let the trout turn down with the fly before lifting the rod and setting the hook.

The biggest problem for the dry-fly angler is avoiding line drag. When fishing across and upstream, you will need to throw an upstream mend of slack line after casting to delay the influence of the current dragging the fly round in an unnatural fashion.

If you are wading, try to get directly downstream of the fish so that the fly drifts down over the fish with the minimum of line drag.

Other Rises

There are many other types of rise which the dry-fly angler will need to learn by observation.

Nebbing rise: This is when the trout pushes its nose right out of the water as heavy hatches of flies hover over its head.

Splashy rise: This is a violent splashing rise which usually happens in the evening when trout are after mayfly or caddis.

Sipping rise: This occurs when insects are trapped in the surface film and usually leaves a bubble behind.

Sub-surface rise: This is the rise that causes all the problems as the trout seems to be rising to take a surface fly, but it is really taking an emerging nymph. As it does so, it disturbs the water making it look like a proper rise.

Head and tail rise: A rise usually seen in smooth stretches of water to nymphs trapped below the surface film where the whole fish appears.

The Trout's View

A trout sees a dry fly from underneath the water, so the wing detail may not be as important as size and colour. The hackles of the dry fly, which make it float, look like the tiny legs of an insect from underwater and trigger the trout to move closer to the surface to investigate. If it is still suspicious, the trout may follow the fly downstream until such time as it either ignores or takes it.

> **IMPORTANT HATCHES**
>
> April: Large dark olive, March brown, yellow Sally. May: Mayfly, iron blue, medium olive. June: Medium olive, pale watery, large stonefly. July: Small dark olive, pale watery, blue-winged olive. August: Sherry spinner, cinnamon sedge, brown silverhorns. September: Autumn dun, caperer, midges.

Above: The observant dry-fly angler learns by experience to recognize the different types of rise that trout commonly make. This will help him to select the correct fly and present it in a manner that the feeding fish will accept.
Left: Once you have selected the correct imitation fly to match those that the trout are taking, position yourself downstream and cast at, but not over, the rising fish.

BANK FISHING – SMALL WATERS

ALTHOUGH MOST small trout waters are now open throughout the year, the natural cycle begins in April when the water starts to warm and the trout move towards the surface in their search for natural food. The fishery manager usually increases his level of fish stocks to match the increased demand from fishermen, and the injection of fresh fish stirs up any resident fish into feeding.

Spring

In spring, the most deadly method of catching fish on the majority of small waters, whatever their depth or clarity, is to use a slow-sinking or clear intermediate line with a brightly coloured marabou-tailed lure, such as a Tadpole, or a heavily leaded 'nymph' like a Montana. During the

day's fishing you may need to change lure colours several times as the fish become more cautious.

Use a single fly on a 12-foot (3.7m) leader of 5lb (2.27kg) breaking strain and vary your retrieves from a slow figure-of-eight to a jerky strip. Always watch your line for takes 'on the drop'. You may see it twitch or straighten out before feeling the pull from a taking trout. The fish will not always hook themselves. You may need to strike by pulling the rod sideways.

Most important of all is first to locate the fish, which may still be in shoals. On a gravel pit this may mean walking the banks, casting every few yards or so until a fish is hooked. Also look for signs of fish splashing or breaking the surface. Once located, you should be able to catch fish easily.

Above: The Goldhead Damsel is arguably the most successful stillwater trout fly. Right: May action with the Damsel nymph on a clear Midlands gravel pit.

TOP TIP

Fishing can be too easy in those early weeks of April and May. You may have to move away from the fish or risk catching your limit too quickly. If you are on a catch-and-release water, do not hog the best spot. Move off and give someone else a chance.

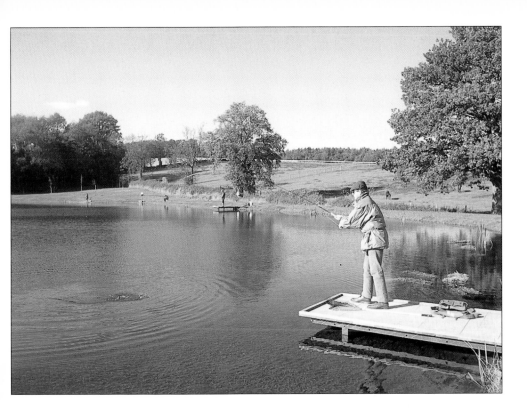

Above: Cool autumn temperatures brings the trout on the feed on small waters. Here casting platforms give access to deeper water.

Summer

As spring warms into summer, the trout will become more selective and you will have to match what they are taking naturally. The Damsel Nymph in all its many forms becomes the number one fly, fished in long strips or with a steady figure-of-eight retrieve on a floating line. All small waters have populations of damsels, and the nymph stage is readily taken by the trout. Some small waters also enjoy a hatch of mayfly, especially if there is a river close by. Then the nymph, emerger or dry Mayfly can work.

As on the larger waters, a hot summer brings its own problems of weed and algae. The trout may become lethargic and refuse to feed. Many fishery owners are reluctant to stock at this time of year, as the trout will feed only at first and last light.

If the weed becomes thick enough to afford the fish cover, it is always worth jiggling a leaded fly under a mat of weed. Trout will lie underneath these natural features during the day for both shelter and food, venturing out into open water only at dusk.

Autumn

With the onset of cooler weather, the fishery manager will often stock his biggest fish. The lures of early season will start to work again, especially with fish that can become aggressive through spawning instincts. However, some rainbows, especially cock fish, become so obsessed with vainly trying to spawn that they will ignore everything thrown at them.

Small leaded patterns, such as the Corixa, or a wet Goldhead Daddy, will work best fished on long, fine leaders. On some days, a dry Daddy may take a fish, while a late hatch of olives will see a small CDC dry working. But take it easy on the strike. This is the time of year when 20-pounders (9kg) are at large.

Winter

This can be a dour time with little obvious activity, except on a warm day when a sudden rise in temperature can see the trout chasing a small lure. Some fisheries now stock triploid trout – fish that have been biologically altered to lose their spawning urges. These sexless rainbows retain their body weight, colour and condition right through the winter.

BANK FISHING – RESERVOIRS

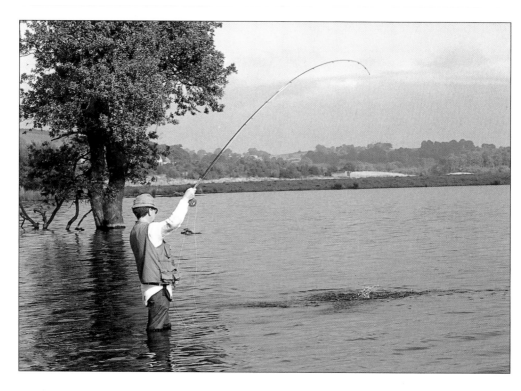

ASTER IS usually the magic date marked on every trout angler's calendar signifying opening day on the reservoirs. We may no longer see the long queues at the lodge to buy a ticket, but from first light every potential space along the banks is usually taken.

Spring

The opening week on any reservoir is a time of plenty with limit bags commonplace as the naive stockfish take any fly cast at them. The bigger resident trout that have overwintered are usually more cautious and need a fly that closely imitates their natural food. But the fish will not be found everywhere on the reservoir; they will usually be concentrated close to the banks in shallow water, or at the base of dam walls. Often the downwind bank will be the most productive, even if casting into the wind cuts down the distance of your cast.

After the winter the water will still be cool, so a sinking line and lure will be your best attack. The most popular method is the Booby fished with a fast-sinking line on a very short leader. This is cast out as far as

Above: Freshly-flooded land on a new reservoir produces rich feeding.

possible, allowed to sink right to the bottom, and then twitched back to the angler with a very slow figure-of-eight retrieve. Takes will be vicious with the Booby often being completely swallowed. That is why the fly is usually banned on waters where catch-and-release is allowed.

Summer

As the water warms up and the natural insects, such as the midge, start to hatch off, the trout turn to natural food. Now is the time for the floating line, long leader and a leaded nymph like a Pheasant Tail or a Buzzer. The fish will feed close to the bank in the early mornings or evenings, moving out of range of the shore angler during the day. The angler will need to find a bank with access to deep water where he can make a long cast, and let the wind blow the line round in an arc. He hardly needs to move the flies; the wind will do all the work. But the leader must be watched like a hawk for the slightest twitch or pull, which must be struck.

By mid-summer, the major fly hatches may have finished and the fishing time is restricted to just the last hour of daylight. Weed rich in natural food will be thick and may make bank fishing almost impossible. Now a small dry fly like a Sedge may be the only way to catch a wary trout.

Autumn

This can be the best time of all on the reservoir with the fish in sparkling condition after months of freedom in the water. Their major food source will now be coarse-fish fry, which they harry and chase around the weedbeds, harbours and boat moorings. This is the time of year when the largest reservoir fish of all are taken.

The favourite technique is to use the Floating Fry, an accurate representation of a fish fry made from Plastazote. This should be cast out into the shallows, or moored off a weedbed, into an area where trout are harrying fry and left unmoved by the angler. The trout may swirl at the fly for several seconds before sucking it down confidently.

The other fly to try is the sinuous Minkie, made from a strip of mink or rabbit fur, and retrieved very slowly on a floating or intermediate line. The fish just appear behind it and suck it in.

Winter

Most reservoirs close their doors at Christmas, giving the hardy bank angler two months additional fishing. With the levels usually lower and the water very clear, fishing is now difficult. Rainbows will still feed in water down to 40°F (5°C), taking small lures on medium-sinking lines. But a warm spell in the middle of the day may mean a hatch of small black midge, and this may bring on a sudden rise. Any brown trout inadvertently hooked after the end of October must be returned.

FAVOURITE FLY COLOURS

Favourite early-season fly colours are green and black, bright orange, white and vivid yellow.

Right: The Booby with its buoyant Plastazote eyes is one of the most successful early-season flies ever devised. In summer, most fly hatches have finished and reservoir bank sport is restricted to morning and evening.

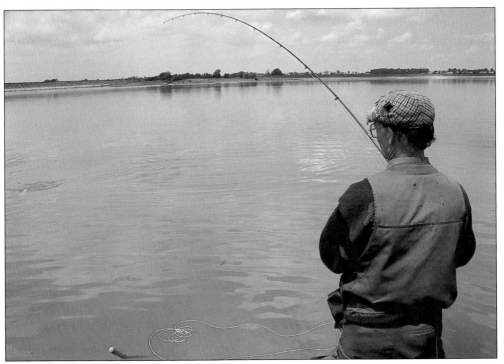

DRY-FLY FISHING – STILLWATER

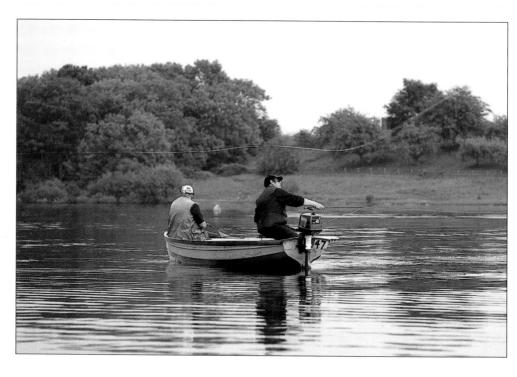

LONG REGARDED as a method for rivers only, modern dry-fly fishing has revolutionized stillwater fishing in the last decade. Anglers on Cambridgeshire's Grafham Water wanted a fly that would take the surface-feeding rainbows in summer as they hunted for insect food trapped in the wind lanes. And they came up with the Emerger, a simple seal's-fur pattern that sat right in the surface film of the water to represent a hatching midge.

Christened Bob's Bits after its creator Bob Worts, this simple dry fly, with its white goose wing for visual sighting, and its host of similar imitations were to change a generation of fly fishermen. Sinking lines and lures were relegated to the bottom of the fishing bag as the whole country went dry-fly crazy.

On a summer's day on a reservoir, every boat angler could be seen dry-fly fishing without one arm being raised for stripping a wet fly. The method spread right around the country, proving as effective in the Highlands of Scotland as on the reservoirs of the West Country.

Reputations and careers in trout fishing were launched on the back of modern dry-fly fishing, as match teams became increasingly better at the art. And although

Above: A flat calm at Bewl Water, Kent, and time for the dry flies.

the method originated in the east of England, it was certainly refined and used to perhaps greatest effect on reservoirs like Chew and Blagdon.

From the original Bits family grew developments like the Raider series of flies, and then the famous Hoppers with bodies of orange, claret, amber, black or olive and pheasant-tail legs. The Hopper must be one of the most important flies of the 1990s.

Sink the Leader

Hoppers can be used even when there is no sign of any rising fish. Provided the trout are within a few feet of the surface, Hoppers will bring the fish up. A tiny smear of floatant, such as Gink, will keep the fly afloat while the leader must be degreased and well sunk by first running it through a degreasing agent like Ledasink.

As with all dry-fly fishing, never be in too much of a hurry to strike. The fish must be allowed sufficient time to take the fly and turn down with it. If you strike too quickly, you will simply pull the fly out of the fish's mouth.

Sometimes the Hopper will be taken with a noisy, splashy rise. But at other times the fish will simply suck it down with scarcely a ripple. Often the Hopper will be taken after being waterlogged and sinking into the wave. The first the angler knows of a take is when he sees the leader straightening out on the surface.

You can also pull the Hopper like a wet fly when the trout are in a chasing mood. Try it on the top dropper of a team of three, and the following trout will often turn down to take the middle or end fly.

Olive Duns

Of course, there are many other more dry flies that work well on the day. And one of the most important is the cul-de-canard (CDC), which represents the lake olive dun which hatches on stillwaters in spring and autumn. The traditional dry pattern for this insect is the Greenwell's Glory, which should still be in every angler's box.

Dry caddis or deer-hair sedge patterns can work well in late summer when the winged insects are active, particularly at dusk. However, when the tiny Caenis flies are smothering the water, it is doubtful if anything will work.

Patterns that imitate terrestrial flies are also important, particularly on upland waters. In spring, you will need a Hawthorn fly for the trout taking the natural hawthorns on the water. Then in summer beetle, flying ant, ladybird and spider patterns will all take their share of fish. Autumn will see craneflies blown out onto the lake when the dry Daddy should work. Fish a single pattern on a long leader and simply let it blow out from the bank with the breeze.

Left: Claret Hopper – one of the most successful dry flies.

Above: The Shuttlecock uses CDC to keep it afloat.
Left: The Cul-de-canard (CDC) Dun works well at olive-hatching time.

MAYFLY PATTERNS

Some stillwaters close by a stream, or fed by alkaline springs, may enjoy a hatch of mayfly. Again patterns like the Silhouette, Shadow Mayfly, Green Drake or Grey Wulff can work on the right day when the duns are hatching.

Right: An evening's flat calm at Leicestershire's Eyebrook Reservoir demands a very careful dry-fly approach. Individual rising fish must be targeted and cast at, without scaring them.

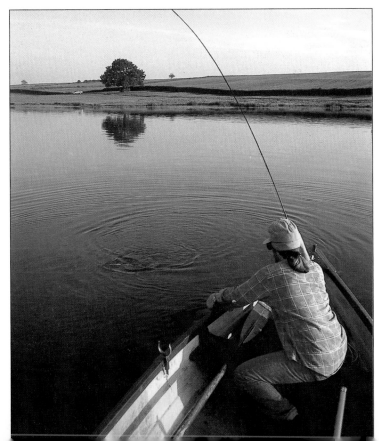

BOAT FISHING – DRIFTING

THIS IS the most popular style of trout fishing in the British Isles, and forms the basis of the many competitions up and down the country. Known as 'loch style' fishing due to its Scottish roots, it involves two anglers casting and retrieving up to three flies in front of a moving boat. The benefit of the style is that large areas of water can be covered in a day.

There are many rules, both written and unwritten, governing this branch of the sport. The most important is to cast only in front of the boat. Even casting in front of the other angler is regarded as unsporting.

In a group of boats, such as a competition, it is important that all the boats drift at the same angle across the waves. Otherwise they will simply cross each other's paths. This is achieved by starting the drifts well away from each other, and with the boat engines all on the same side, usually on the anglers' left.

Equally important, at the end of the drift, is not to motor up or across another boat's drift. This is regarded as bad manners and causes a lot of ill feeling on the reservoirs. Similarly, bank anglers feel aggrieved when a boat drifts right on top of them when they are catching fish.

All boat anglers like a light breeze and gentle ripple to blow them along. If the wind is not too strong, they can fish dry flies and nymphs on floating lines, often cast to fish they can see moving on the surface of the water.

Fishing three wet flies on a floating line can be exciting, especially when the fish chase the flies right up to the boat. It is then that skill takes over, as the angler has only a second or two to tease the chasing trout into taking his flies.

When the wind gets up, a brake in the form of a drogue is needed to slow the boat down. This is attached

---

TOP TIP

If you hook a fish in open water, take a bearing and return to the same spot on your next drift, even if it is short. The shoal will not be far away.

Left: Here, the angler in the bows has hooked a trout at Kent's Bewl Water during match practice.

Above: Mini lures, such as this Peach Crystal Doll, are an important part of loch-style competition fishing. Lures like this are usually fished on the point of a three-fly cast.

FLIES

• Wets: Soldier Palmer, Grenadier, Pearly Wickhams, Silver Invicta, Mallard and Claret, Oakham Orange, Black Pennell.

• Dries: Claret Hopper, Shipman's Buzzer, Bob's Bits, Suspender Buzzer, Red Emerger, CDC Dun.

• Nymphs: Gold-ribbed Hare's Ear, Diawl Bach, Epoxy Buzzer, Deer-hair Midge, Hot-spot Pheasant Tail, Green-tag Stickfly.

• Lures: Peach Doll, Jungle Cock Viva, mini Appetizer, Light Bulb, mini Muddler, Cat's Whisker.

Above: This splendid Chew rainbow has fallen to a small Floating Fry.

Below: Loch-style competition is an area of fly fishing that is growing in popularity.

to the gunnel of the boat behind the angler, usually with a small G-clamp attached to an inverted rowlock, and thrown out into the wind and water. It acts like an underwater parachute and consequently slows the boat's progress.

On windy, cool days, the anglers may need to use sinking lines, from the very fast-sinking Di-7 line up to a clear intermediate line which sinks just under the surface. Finding the depth at which the fish are feeding is all part of the art.

If the fish are lying deep, then a long cast with a fast-sinking line is required and enough time should be allowed before starting the retrieve to let the line to sink down to them. This is an art in itself, and the successful angler needs to take up just sufficient slack to stay in touch with the flies, yet permitting the line to sink deep enough for the fish. Often the trout will follow the flies up to the surface, taking only at the last moment 'on the hang' when the angler stops retrieving and lets the flies hang in the water ten feet (3m) or so down.

Tackle

You will need a 10ft (3m) 6/7 weight rod; a three-fly 15ft (4.6m) leader; a forward-taper floater, intermediate, medium sinking; fast-sinking lines; a boat seat and drogue.

BOAT FISHING – TROLLING/ANCHORING

ALTHOUGH DRIFTING may often be the most sporting way of fly fishing from a boat, invariably the largest fish fall to trolling or anchoring. The first method involves using the boat to move the fly, either on the engine or the oars. This allows long lengths of line to be let out so the fly is able to sink to great depths. Also large areas of water can be covered while the fly is always moving at a continuous speed.

Although popular in Ireland and Scotland, the method is regarded as so deadly for catching stocked rainbow trout that it is banned on most English reservoirs. However, there are legal ways around this. The first is to use a rudder, and the second is to lock the oars in the rowlocks. Both methods then take advantage of the wind to propel the boat along bowfirst.

Two anglers can fish, one on either side of the boat, taking it in turns to cast and allowing the fly to swing around in an arc behind the boat. The takes often come as the fly accelerates round. This method is known as the 'Northampton' style after the area where anglers first pioneered it.

TOP TIP

Look for gulls feeding on coarse fish fry driven to the surface. The trout will be beneath them.

Without a rudder or locked oars, the boat would simply turn sideways-on to the wind and drift too slowly for the fly to be effective. Even so, the method is still allowed only on certain reservoirs, such as Rutland and Draycote. Rudders are banned at Grafham, although locked oars are permitted. Windy days are best to drive the boat along. But be careful not to be driven onto the dam.

Tackle

You will need a heavyish, 8/9 weight, 10ft (3m) rod, a wide-drummed reel with either a shooting head of lead-cored line or a full Hi-D. On some days when the fish are high in the wave, a medium-sinking line like a Wet Cel 2 works best.

Below: Anchoring late season at Gaynes Cove, Grafham Water.

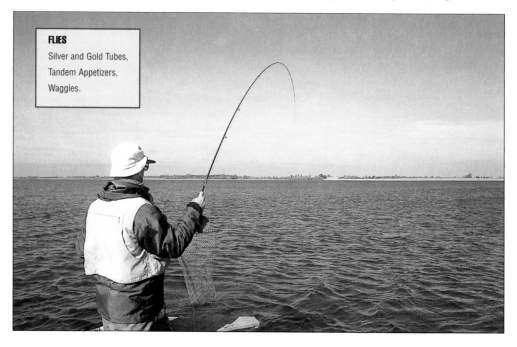

FLIES
Silver and Gold Tubes, Tandem Appetizers, Waggies.

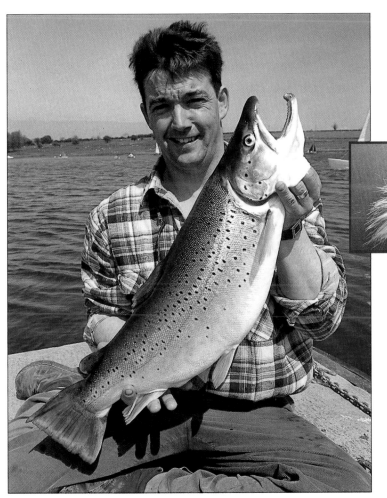

FLIES

White, Yellow or Viva
Boobies, Razzler, Hare's
Ear, Pheasant Tail
Nymph, Epoxy Buzzer,
Corixa, Sedge Pupa.

Above: Dan's Fry.

TOP TIP

Always pull up the
anchor from the bows,
never from the side of
the boat. If it gets
stuck, motor upwind
of the anchor position
and pull from there. It
also pays to 'trip' the
anchor before you put
it down.

Anchoring

Early season on the reservoir will often find the trout
shoaled up in a bay close to the bank. This is the time to
drop the anchor and fish a lure or Booby on a fast-sinking
line. With the wind behind you, you can cast right into the
bank, provided no bank angler is there first.

Always make sure that the anchor rope is tied securely
to the boat before dropping it over the side. Then after you
have let out sufficient rope, make a loop in it and attach it
to the rowlock, so two anglers can fish broadside.

Do not have too sharp an angle in the rope. This is
dangerous if the wind gets up and water starts to splash
into the boat. Let out sufficient so that the anchor chain is
flat on the bottom. If it becomes too windy to fish
broadside, you will have to anchor the boat from the bow
and take it in turns to cast from the stern.

Above: A grown-on, double-figure brown trout from Rutland Water.

By gradually letting out more anchor rope, you can
cover fresh ground. But the boat will swing around in the
water more. Serious boat anglers take two anchors, and use
one from the stern and one from bow to keep the boat
steady.

Tackle

Anchoring allows you to fish your flies as slowly as you
like, so flies like the Booby or general nymphs are best. A
fast-sinking line, such as a Hi-D with a short leader, will
work best early season; a floating line and a long leader in
summer. It could pay you to use a plumb line to find the
depth of the water before you fish. About 10 to 12 feet (3-
3.7m) is generally best.

STALKING

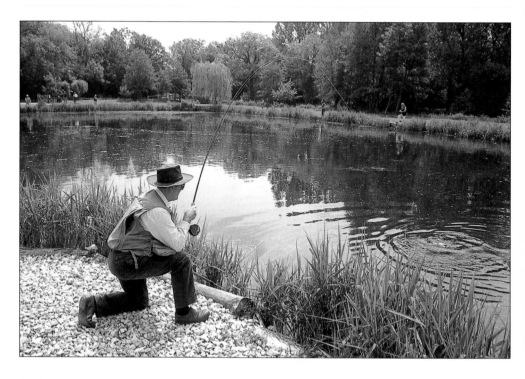

THE POPULARITY of stalking grew with the opening of small stillwaters, stocked with large fish, that were clear enough for the angler to see his quarry. Most of these venues are concentrated in the south of England where clear chalk-stream water feeds the lakes, and is not affected by winter rain. However, stalking is an effective method on any trout water where the angler can see his fish.

Getting Started

The most essential item of tackle is a good pair of Polaroid sunglasses, followed by a wide-brimmed hat. The sunglasses will allow the angler to see through the reflected surface glare on the water, while the hat will keep any unwanted sunlight out of his eyes. Only by wearing these will the angler be able to spot his quarry.

The flies must be heavily weighted so that they sink quickly to the level of the fish. The water is invariably deeper than you think, and the fly takes longer to get down than anticipated. It will also pay you to have a spot of colour somewhere on the fly so that you can see it at all times.

Above: Dever Springs, Hampshire, is a top trout-stalking water.

The rod needs to be fairly soft so that the fly can be flicked out easily with the minimum of fly-line beyond the tip ring. This is difficult to achieve with a fast-taper rod.

The leader needs to be short, say eight or nine feet (2.4-2.7m) in length, so that the fly can be worked into position or jiggled in front of a fish. Keep it well rubbed with de-greaser so that the fly sinks easily.

Also make sure that your landing net is large enough to land a trout of double figures. Most top stalkers prefer to use a gye net carried across the back.

Tactics

Make sure that you are at the lake early as the fish stocked the night before will be the easiest to catch. Tackle up

FAVOURITE FLIES

When All Else Fails, Wobble Worm, Red Spot Shrimp, Olive Nobbler, Lead Bug, Hare's Ear Shrimp, Walker Mayfly Nymph, Yellow Corixa.

correctly, as a big fish will use its weight to try to break the line. Weed can also be a problem as the trout will invariably head straight for the nearest weed bed.

Some trout will prove almost impossible to tempt. These are fish that have seen many flies, and may have even been hooked in the past. But do not give up. Keep swapping fly patterns, colours and sizes until you find the one it is prepared to take. It may also pay to drop down to a finer leader. But in any case, use a clear polymer double strength, or one of the new fluorocarbons.

During the day, the light may make it difficult to spot more fish. Try moving to an area of shadow where you can still see beneath the water. Around midday, many fish will move into the weed to hide. Take a break then, conserving your concentration for later in the afternoon when the fish start to move again.

Where You Can Stalk Trout

Any fishery clear enough to allow you to see into the margins. Favourites are Avington and Dever Springs in Hampshire; Chalk Springs in Sussex.

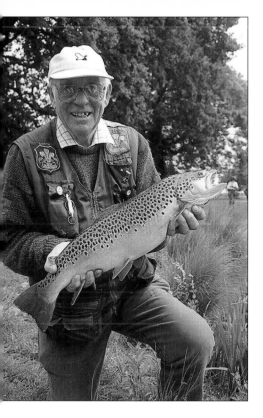

Above: Specimen brownies can be individually targeted in clear water.

TOP TIP

Trout cruise regularly along the margins. Cast your fly out first, and wait until the fish returns. Then swiftly lift the fly off the bottom in front of the trout. It should take the fly instinctively.

before you walk around the lake. You can even hold the fly in your left-hand fingers, ready to 'catapult cast' it at a fish.

Not all the trout you see will be feeding fish. You may have to cast repeatedly at a particular fish for an hour or more before it decides to take the fly out of aggression. Make sure the trout actually sees your fly, and does not swim straight past it. You need to get the fly right in front of its nose, and then pull it away sharply. This is known as inducing the take.

The only way you will know that the trout has taken the fly is when you see the white inside of its open mouth, the fins stiffen and the gills flare. Strike immediately by tightening the line, but make sure the reel drag is set

Right: Orange Lead Bug – a fly specifically for stalking. A double-figure rainbow from Dever Springs for Tony Dixon.

THE WATER

RIVERS

Chalkstreams

Rich in weed and invertebrate life, the fast-flowing chalkstream presents an ideal habitat for the trout. Spring-fed by water that has percolated through porous limestone hills, the classic English chalkstreams rarely flood or colour up, maintaining their clarity and flow right through the year.

Traditionally the home of wild brown trout, many of our classic chalkstreams, like Hampshire's River Test, have been stocked with rainbows to provide easier fishing for anglers prepared to pay heavily for a day ticket. The brown trout, too, are now often stocked, with only a few chalkstreams, such as Dorset's River Piddle, maintaining their truly wild stock.

The alkaline water of the chalkstream encourages a diverse breeding population of water insects, such as the upwinged flies on which our modern river dry-fly fishing

is based. The most famous is the mayfly *(Ephemera danica)* which has enthralled flyfishermen for centuries. When they first hatch in late May, the trout throw caution to the wind and take them with abandon. This glorious time is traditionally known as 'Duffer's fortnight'. However, it does not last and after a few weeks of a mayfly diet, the trout switch off and become increasingly more difficult to catch.

Below: Cumbria's River Greta – a typical north of England freestone river. Here the brown trout are also stocked.

> **TOP CHALKSTREAMS**
>
> Rivers Test, Itchen, Avon, Hampshire; Rivers Dove, Wye and Lathkill, Derbyshire; Rivers Piddle and Frome, Dorset; River Kennet, Berkshire; River Colne, Gloucestershire.

snowmelt, the fast-flowing, moorland headwaters of these rivers are the natural home of wild brown trout that may still be only a few inches long after several years.

However, as the river loses altitude and widens on its headlong flight to the sea, richer feeding becomes available in the form of shrimps, stonefly, caddis, minnows, terrestrial flies and beetles producing brown trout of a pound (0.45kg) or so. The odd, individual fish that turn on to a high-protein diet of minnows, bullheads or even baby trout may reach 3lb (1.36kg) or more.

Although some freestone rivers may be stocked, to a limited degree, at the start of the season by a controlling angling club, the fish are generally left to breed in the wild. Here, the wet fly rules with traditional spider patterns fished on a cast of three being the standard method. These fish can be much more canny to catch than their chalkstream cousins, often only rising at dusk to a hatch of upwinged flies like the March brown *(Rhithrogena germanica)* or Autumn dun *(Ecdyonurus dispar).*

Many of the top salmon and sea-trout rivers of the British Isles also hold good numbers of brown trout that are rarely exploited by flyfishermen. Scotland's River Tweed is one well-known example.

Above: The Derbyshire Wye is a famous chalk stream.

Right: The exclusive River Test now allows grayling fishing.

Other important chalkstream upwinged flies are the blue-winged olive *(Ephemerella ignita)*, large dark olive *(Baetis rhodani)*, small dark olive *(Baetis scambus)*, pale watery *(Baetis fuscatus)* and iron blue dun *(Baetis niger)*. But the sedge or caddis flies are also important in summer.

The first weeks of chalkstream fishing are usually upstream dry-fly only, but nymph fishing is normally permitted from June onwards with classic patterns, such as the Grey Goose, Sawyer's Pheasant Tail and Gold-Ribbed Hare's Ear, imitating the nymph stage of the upwinged flies. Again these are normally fished upstream, dead drift, watching the leader like a hawk for takes.

Then as summer slips into autumn, and grayling come into the picture, the weighted Killer Bug takes its toll of these handsome fish. Grayling used to be considered a pest on chalkstreams. Now they are a popular quarry.

Freestone Rivers

Wild rivers with rapids, shallows, riffles, pools and pockets help make the landscape of northern and western Britain some of the most beautiful in Europe. Fed by rain or

TOP FREESTONE RIVERS

Rivers Wharfe, Ure and Aire, Yorkshire; Rivers Ribble, Hodder and Lune, Lancashire; River Derwent, Derbyshire; Rivers Eden, Greta and Derwent, Cumbria; River Wear, Co Durham; Rivers Tyne and Till, Northumberland; Rivers Exe, Barle, Taw, Torridge and Dart, Devon; Rivers Tweed, Tay, Spey, Dee and Findhorn, Scotland; Rivers Wye, Teifi, Tywi, Dyfi and Dee, Wales.

RESERVOIRS

THE STOCKING of rainbow and brown trout into English reservoirs since the 1960s was a major step in making fly fishing accessible for all. Before then, fly fishing had been regarded as something of an elitist sport for retired colonels and public schoolboys with access to exclusive stretches of chalkstreams.

Two famous reservoirs that have been stocked with brown trout since Victorian times are Blagdon in Somerset, and Ravensthorpe in Northamptonshire. But stocking in those days was at a very low level when compared to today.

The reservoir that changed our flies and tactics was 3,000-acre (1,214ha) Grafham Water in Cambridgeshire, which first opened to flyfishermen in 1966. The newly flooded banks provided a wealth of food for the foraging trout, which grew fast in the nutrient-rich water. Anglers fishing on that opening day quickly found that their tackle was just not up to the strength and power of rainbows of five and six pounds (2.27-2.72kg).

FAMOUS LOWLAND RESERVOIRS

Grafham Water, Cambridgeshire; Rutland Water, Rutland; Eyebrook, Leicestershire; Hanningfield, Essex; Draycote Water, Warwickshire; Blagdon and Chew, Somerset; Bewl Water, Kent; Pitsford, Northamptonshire; Farmoor, Oxon; Llandegfedd, Wales.

Below: Rutland Water is now England's most famous trout-fishing reservoir.

Below inset: Eyebrook in Leicestershire offers tranquil and attractive bank fishing.

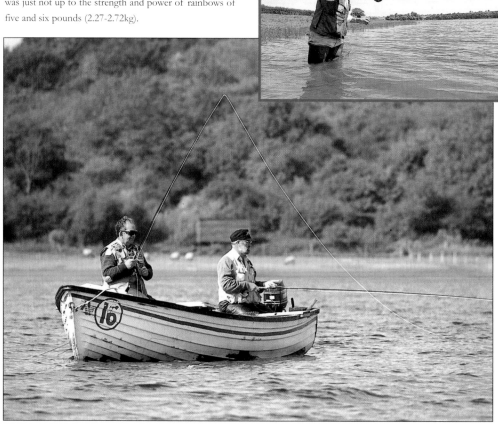

The next few years were spent in developing tackle and flies specifically for reservoir fishing. We saw the birth of the shooting head for distance casting; line baskets to carry the backing; more powerful rods; wider-drummed reels; larger landing nets and a whole host of famous lures, such as the Sweeny Todd, Jack Frost, Black Chenille and Baby Doll, that imitate the dense shoals of coarse-fish fry which the trout preyed upon.

The reservoir revolution brought its own celebrities, with anglers like Bob Church, Dick Shrive and Arthur Cove becoming household angling names. The Northampton-style of boat fishing was born at Grafham, along with modern nymph fishing methods for the bank angler. Specialist dry-fly methods were to follow as anglers learned how to imitate the massive midge hatches that are such a feature of lowland reservoirs. Deep-water techniques using fast-sinking lines and mini-lures were developed for daphnia-feeding trout, while specimen hunters targeted Grafham's giant brown trout with tandem and tube flies up to five inches (12.7cm) long.

Booby fishing followed from the dam wall, a method that was to revolutionize 'concrete bowl' fishing.

Other famous reservoirs such as Rutland and Bewl Water were to open in the following years. Each was to make its mark with its own particular methods and flies, but Grafham's place in fly-fishing history remains unique.

Below: Nant Y Moch Reservoir in West Wales offers traditional boat fishing for stocked and wild brown trout.

Upland Reservoirs

Water companies traditionally built reservoirs in the higher parts of the country where there was plenty of rain. Wales, the North West and the West Country are full of small moorland reservoirs that hold stocks of trout to some degree or another.

Many of these reservoirs are simply too acidic or lacking in food for the trout to put on weight naturally. So they have to be regularly stocked through the season. However, where the trout are able to feed on small fish, such as minnows or sticklebacks, they can still become naturalized.

One solution is to stock with brown trout only, as these fish are naturally able to cope better with colder winters, higher altitude and a mainly terrestrial food source. And several reservoirs, such as Carsington, Elan Valley, Roadford and Colliford, have successfully done just that.

Out-and-out lure techniques are more important at these waters where stocked rainbows are the main quarry. But when wild brownies are sought, the angler will need to be every bit as skillful as the river or loch angler pursuing fish that have bred naturally.

Dry flies that represent terrestrial insects, such as beetles, ants or crane flies, must be cast behind every boulder, or in every bay, to bring up the brown trout boiling on the surface.

FAMOUS UPLAND RESERVOIRS
Wimbleball, Somerset; Roadford, Devon; Colliford, Cornwall; Leighton and Washburn Valley, Yorkshire; Derwent, Co Durham; Kielder, Northumberland; Carsington, Derbyshire; Stocks, Lancashire; Clywedog, Elan Valley, Llyn Brenig, Wales.

NATURAL LAKES

To FIND natural trout lakes in the British Isles, you must travel to either Scotland, Wales, Ireland or the Lake District. These stretches of water created in the Ice Age are the natural home of brown trout, and also of salmon and sea-trout if connected to the sea.

The richest and largest lakes are in the west of Ireland where the alkaline water encourages a wealth of insect life, including mayfly. Here the brown trout grow big and fat with wild double-figure fish caught every season.

The more acidic waters are the Highland lochs where some stunted browns may be many years old. However, if they turn predatory at an early age and become ferox trout, they can grow to more than 20lb (9kg). The richer Scottish waters, such as Loch Leven, are in the lowlands, where a

certain amount of eutrophication has enriched the water so helping the wild trout to put on weight. Rainbows stocked here at a few ounces often achieve double-figure weights.

Most of the natural trout lakes in Wales have now been turned into reservoirs, although conservation areas like Snowdon have a number of mountain llyns supporting wild browns. A similar situation occurs in the English Lake District. However, overall, wild brown trout are a threatened species.

Small Stillwaters

To cater for the growing demand for trout fishing, all types of water have been stocked with trout – although not all are suitable! The best and most popular are those clearwater fisheries fed by chalk springs where the fish can be spotted and individually stalked. These are mainly concentrated in the south of England where there are natural trout streams close by. Elsewhere, many of our underused gravel pits have been pressed into service as

TOP NATURAL LAKES
Loughs Corrib, Conn, Mask and Sheelin, Eire; Loughs Erne and Melvin, Ulster; Lochs Leven, Garry, Hope, Watten, Rannoch and Awe, Scotland; Lakes Windermere, Coniston and Buttermere, Cumbria; Malham Tarn, Yorkshire; Lakes Tal-y-llyn, Bugeilyn, Gregennan, Wales.

Below: A natural lake high in Snowdonia National Park.

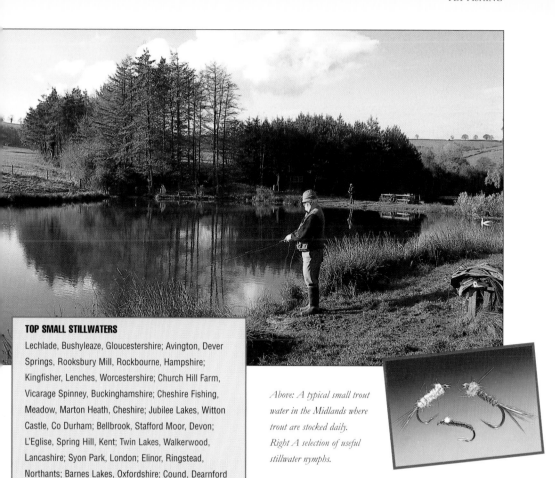

Above: A typical small trout water in the Midlands where trout are stocked daily.
Right A selection of useful stillwater nymphs.

trout fisheries. Their naturally clear water, rich weed growth and variation in depth make them ideal fisheries with good growing potential.

Some of the best-known gravel pit fisheries are concentrated along the Thames valley, but you will also find them along the Nene, Ouse and Bure valleys in Eastern England. Many old estate lakes in the Midlands have been stocked with trout, while the home counties are dotted with small lakes and ponds now turned over to trout. Disused reservoirs, quarries and clay pits make up many of the north's best-known stillwater fisheries, but more and more fishery owners are now turning to digging out their own 'designer' lakes. However, many small fisheries in the south have suffered from drought and high temperatures in recent summers, leading to some fish deaths, lice infestation, heavy weeding and temporary closure.

Wales and Scotland are rich in natural stillwaters, and these two areas have seen a massive growth in new fisheries in recent years.

The most successful small waters are those that are fed by a natural spring or small stream which can keep the water temperature down and the oxygen supply up in hot weather. Stocked rainbow trout are remarkably tenacious, but when the water temperature climbs above 68°F (20°C) like humans they will become lethargic and go right off the feed.

Many smallwaters hold an unnaturally high stock of fish with insufficient food to maintain the biomass. Thus the average life expectancy of a trout may be only two to three days. Many fishery owners have to resort to feeding their trout artificially in the winter.

INDEX